Travel with your Family

Experts Share Their Secrets

REUNIONS & VACATIONS
With Grandparents,
Grandkids,
Siblings,
In-laws, and
The Rest of the Gang!

Fodor'sfyi

Fodor's Travel Publications
New York • Toronto • London • Sydney • Auckland
www.fodors.com

Editors: Karen Cure, Deborah Kaufman
Managing Editors: Robin Dellabough, Lisa DiMona, Karen Watts
Editorial Contributors: John Stone, Caroline Haberfeld
Production/Manufacturing: Publications Development Company of Texas
Cover Design: Guido Caroti
Interior Design: Lisa Sloane

A Lark Production

Copyright © 2002 by Fodors LLC

Fodor's is a registered trademark of Random House, Inc.

All rights reserved under International and Pan-American Copyright Conventions. Published in the United States by Fodor's Travel Publications, a unit of Fodors LLC, a subsidiary of Random House, Inc., and simultaneously in Canada by Random House of Canada Limited, Toronto. Distributed by Random House, Inc., New York.

No portion of this book may be reproduced in any form without written permission from the publisher.

First Edition

ISBN: 1-4000-1159-0

Important Tip

Although all details in this book are based on information supplied to us at press time, changes occur all the time in the travel world, and Fodor's cannot accept responsibility for facts that become outdated or for inadvertent errors or omissions. So always confirm information when it matters.

Special Sales

Fodor's Travel Publications are available at special discounts for bulk purchases for sales promotions or premiums. Special editions, including personalized covers, excerpts of existing guides, and corporate imprints, can be created in large quantities for special needs. For more information, contact your local bookseller or write to Special Markets, Fodor's Travel Publications, 280 Park Avenue, New York, NY 10017. Inquiries from Canada should be directed to your local Canadian bookseller or sent to Random House of Canada, Ltd., Marketing Department, 2775 Matheson Boulevard East, Mississauga, Ontario L4W 4P7. Inquiries from the United Kingdom should be sent to Fodor's Travel Publications, 20 Vauxhall Bridge Road, London SW1V 2SA, England.

Printed in the United States of America

10 9 8 7 6 5 4 3 2 1

Contents

HAVE FAMILY, WILL TRAVEL	**1**
Laying the Groundwork	3

1 VACATION CREATION:	
GETTING STARTED	**5**

The Travel Planner 7
Choosing the Planner 7 *Do You Have What It Takes to Be the Travel Planner?* 8 Sharing the Role 9 Taking Charge 9 Consider a Travel Professional 10 *How to Pick a Travel Agent* 11 All Aboard: Who is Going? 12 *Family Travel Survey* 13 Family Planning Meetings 14 *A Teleconference* 15 *A Chat Room* 16 Countdown to Travel 17 *A Planning Timeline* 18

A Family Reunion 20
Don't Go It Alone 20 *Tracing Family Roots* 21

Going as a Grandparent 21
Physical Challenges 22 Who's in Charge? 25 Grandparents and Grandchildren Together 25

First Steps with Steps and In-Laws 26
The Awkwardness Factor 28 *Ex-Spouses and Your Children's Needs* 29

Traveling in a Nontraditional Family 31
Proclaim Your Identity 32

Benefit from the Unexpected 32

2 THE TRAVEL BUDGET — 34

Reaching a Comfort Level 35
Finding Deals 36   *Measuring Family Means* 37
Accommodating Different Budgets 38
Affordability Equals Happiness 40   *Estimate At-Home Expenses* 41   *Family Budget Planner* 42
Turn on Your Calculator 44

Putting Together the Trip 45
Getting the Most for Your Money 45   *How to Get Great Rates: Questions to Explore* 46   *Back Up Your Records* 50   Handling the Money 51   *The Usual Conditions in Brochures* 53   Handling Travel Complaints 55

Identifying Hidden Costs 56
All-Inclusives vs. Noninclusives 57   *Deceptive Prices* 57   *What's Not Included?* 58   Maid Service 60   *A Good Deal or a Bad One?* 61   Taxes, Service Charges, Extras 61   Prearranged Tours and Packages 62

The Family Angel 63
When Your Relative Pays 64   Expressing Gratitude 66

3 PLACES TO GO, THINGS TO DO — 68

What Kind of Destination 69
Comparing Surveys 69   *What Appeals to You?* 70
What's Your Travel Style? 71   Go-Goers 72
Culture Vultures 72   Relaxation Gurus 73

Sports and Adventure Enthusiasts 73   No-Hands Fans 74

Choosing a Destination 74
Resources 75   Narrowing Down Your Choices 77   *How to Pick a Destination* 78

Vacation Ideas 78
City Vacations 78   *12 Splendid Cities You'll Love* 80   Beach Vacations 81   *A Bouquet of Beaches—Pick One* 82   A Touring Trip 84   Cruises 87   Theme Parks 93   *A Theme Park Wherever You Are* 98   Winter Sports Vacations 99   *Winter Resorts to Consider* 101   Camping and Hiking 103   *Campground Etiquette* 104   *10 Great Options Outdoors* 105

Alternative Vacations 107
City Slickers on Open Prairies 107   Bonding on the Fairway 108   *The Front Nine: Top Golf Getaways* 109   River Rafting 110   Volunteering 110   *10 Great Rivers Worth Rafting* 111

4 GETTING THE SHOW ON THE ROAD   113

Air Travel 114
Sharing Frequent Flier Awards 115   Airport Shuttle 115   *Required Travel Documents* 116   At the Airport 117   *Children's Onboard Survival Kits* 119

The Rubber-Tire Vacation 119
Essentials for Your Car 120   The Navigator 120   Rendezvous Stops 121   Family Car Games 121   Breaking up the Trip 122   *Rental Car Extras to Price Out* 123   Rent a Car or a Van? 124

Travel by Ship 124

Pros and Cons of Coach Tours 126

Your Own Driver-Guide 127

Travel by Train 129

---

5 HOME AWAY FROM HOME   **130**

Hotels, Resorts, and B&Bs 131
Lodging Comforts You May Want 132   Family-Friendly or Not? 133   *Evaluating Children's Programs* 134   The Right Price 135   Executive Floors 137   Reunion Space 138   Coping with Front-Desk Delays 138

Family Vacation Rentals 139
Finding a House 140   *Rental Comforts You May Want* 141   Get It in Writing 143   *What to Note in Rental Paperwork* 145   On Vacation: Cleanup and Kitchen Duties 146

Cruise Accommodations 148

---

6 THE GANG'S ALL HERE   **151**

All Together Now 152
How to Decide on Activities Once You Arrive 153   *Sample Reunion Weekend* 156   By the Beach or In the Country 157   Cruises 160   City Time 162

The Children's Hours 165
Kids on their Own 166   With Grandkids 168

The Party's Over: Time to Leave 170
Make Your Memories Last 170   Fond Farewells 171   Going Home Happy 173

RESOURCES   **176**

Have Family, Will Travel

WHEN WAS THE LAST TIME YOU AND YOUR WHOLE family gathered together—parents and grandparents, sisters and brothers, aunts and uncles, nieces and nephews, cousins and in-laws? At a wedding last year? A graduation ceremony three years ago? Thanksgiving 1987? Rounding up the entire crew can be difficult, particularly if your family members are scattered across the country. And the usual gatherings can be unsatisfying: a flurry of activity, your attention divided among a dozen people, brief snatches of conversation before someone has to baste the turkey and stir the gravy. Are you looking to spend some serious, power-bonding quality time with your family? Then you may be in the market for an extended-family vacation.

Think of it as a two-for-one deal. You get the pleasure of traveling—a break from work or school, new surroundings, exciting activities, good food, and unusual discoveries—plus the companionship of relatives you've hoped to see more often. And you may come to understand your extended family in a whole new light.

Maybe you've been considering such a vacation for a while. Maybe you got the idea when you returned from a conference or a trip to a faraway island. Maybe your children or grandchildren inspired you with tales of lands they've been studying in school. Whatever sparked your imagination, hold on to the idea: arranging an extended-family vacation may seem like a daunting task, but a carefully thought-out plan can turn your vision into reality.

Sure, you'll face challenges: an extended-family vacation requires much more work than planning a trip for your immediate family. First of all, your relatives will all have to agree on a destination, mode of transportation, and type of lodging. As with any group, the more people who join, the harder it will be to reach a consensus. You'll have to reconcile different budgets, different schedules, and different interests to bring everyone together. And making the arrangements for large groups—from booking airline seats and hotel rooms to reserving space for family parties—requires a lot of advance preparation.

Just thinking about the details involved can hold you back if you let it. But good planning and lots of family participation can help you hurdle the stumbling blocks. And the rewards of an extended-family vacation far outweigh the efforts of planning it. You'll catch up with distant family members you haven't seen in years. You can see for yourself—instead of in the annual holiday photograph—how your relatives' children have grown. The younger members of the family may form life-long friendships. The leisurely rhythms of vacation allow room for experiences that will become part of your family lore and create memories you'll treasure for years to come. And best of all, you may start a brand-new family tradition.

LAYING THE **GROUNDWORK**

So maybe your family is wild for a trip together, but no one knows how to begin. One family member needs to step up to the plate, take charge, and convert your enthusiasm into a structured plan.

Maybe that person is you. Maybe it's a family member close to you who simply needs your support to get started. Whoever takes charge, the first step is to encourage everyone else in the family to bring all their ideas to the designated family travel planner. Involving everyone, from kids to grandparents, in the process of gathering ideas will not only produce the best family vacation but just may produce a trip so magical that your extended family decides to repeat the entire process again next year.

Once the ideas start flowing and solidifying, you'll need to plan carefully—and plan just about everything, from booking an airport shuttle to arranging the farewell dinner. The pages that follow will help you to get started with your preparations, to work out a budget, choose a destination, and to figure out how to make the most of your family time together.

The Editors

Vacation Creation: Getting Started

MAYBE YOUR FANTASY FAMILY VACATION goes something like this: the little ones quietly build lopsided sandcastles while the adults look on benignly from pink lounge chairs, exchanging reminiscences as they sip piña coladas capped with miniature umbrellas. Off in the distance, the teenagers play beach volleyball and ride the waves (but still remember to check in with their parents every half hour). Later on, at the campfire, three generations roast gooey marshmallows, tell stories, remember past family gatherings, and anticipate an upcoming wedding or celebration.

Does it sound too good to be true? Well, it probably is. Consider what's missing: your daughter pouring a bucket of water over her older brother's head; your uncle, in his lime green bathing suit, croaking out "Under the Boardwalk"; your cousin's dog trying to join the volleyball game; and all the little idiosyncrasies that make your family *your* family. These images may never make the cover of *Travel + Leisure,* but the truth is your family vacation wouldn't be the same without them. And the reality may even be better than the fantasy. So scrap the Walton-family-vacation fantasy and start putting plans together for a trip with that lovable, quirky group that is your real family.

Sure, there will be kinks to work out: your father is afraid to fly, and your mother gets carsick. Aunt Gertrude and Aunt Marcy can't be in the same room for more than five minutes without fighting. Your kids don't want to leave their fish behind. No one said gathering your extended family together would be simple. But with some careful planning and contributions from all of your family members, it doesn't have to be hard.

If you haven't already discussed your vacation idea with your relatives, you'll need to contact some influential members of your extended family and organize a meeting by phone or in person. Toss around some ideas and suggestions. You'll quickly get an idea of whether anyone shares your enthusiasm. And if other family members do, your first step will be to appoint a travel planner.

THE TRAVEL PLANNER

Now what? Ideas start to fly. Aunt Mildred suggests Mexico, your brother argues for a road trip, your kids beg to go to a theme park, and visions of tropical isles sweep through your mind. Someone in your family has to harness these ideas, help the family agree on key issues, and make the arrangements. In short, someone has to take on the role of head honcho or travel planner.

Choosing the Planner

Family members have different lives, jobs, obligations, and time pressures. Helping them overcome the obstacles that block the way to your extended-family trip is a complicated but rewarding job, requiring organization; understanding at some times; firmness at others; flexibility, management skills, and creativity. Discuss what the travel-planner role will require and which family member seems most qualified and most willing. Whomever you choose, agree that he or she will be in charge of putting the trip together. There will be plenty of opportunities for everyone to

DO YOU HAVE WHAT IT TAKES TO BE THE TRAVEL PLANNER?

- [ ] Do you want to be the planner?
- [ ] Do you have the time to put into the project?
- [ ] Have you had travel experience?
- [ ] Did you plan your own trips?
- [ ] Are you organized?
- [ ] Do you keep good notes and records?
- [ ] Are you good with accounts and credit cards?
- [ ] How are your shopping skills? Can you find and negotiate the best values?
- [ ] Do you have good communication skills?
- [ ] Do you have access to a fax, a copying machine, and a computer with E-mail?

contribute, but things will go more smoothly if one person oversees it all.

Have your family agree on some kind of small reward or thanks for the travel planner. (It shouldn't be a totally thankless job.) Putting this vacation together will take a lot of effort, and he or she deserves a token of appreciation from the family. Maybe you can chip in to cover the cost of one night's accommodations or perhaps even his or her airfare.

Sharing the Role

As the travel planner you'll be in charge, but you won't have to do it alone. Draw on your own family members and their various skills for support. Perhaps your strength is financial record keeping, but you're less comfortable communicating with people. As the travel planner, you can enlist one or two people to assist with details. Then designate a sales-skilled helper to communicate and negotiate. If management is your strength, but you don't want to handle money, assign a banker. Or consider appointing an entertainment director to organize family activities at your destination. Whatever the arrangement, you, the travel planner, are in charge.

Agree on a representative for each participating household in your extended family. Have the representative speak to each member of his or her household to gather ideas and communicate them to the head planner. Your brother, for example, might be the representative for himself and his wife and children. Your mother might speak for both of your parents. The children might decide that one of their brothers or sisters can relay what the kids would like to do on the trip.

Taking Charge

As the travel planner your job is to take responsibility for coordinating the trip and working with the travel companies that will serve your family. Limit yourself to one or two assistant planners and rely on the household representatives to convey your needs and ideas to the different members of your extended family as they prepare with you for the trip. Remember to be fair and flexible. This is a family vacation, not a business operation. You've been put in charge to facilitate matters for the whole family, not to hand down your decisions to the rest of your family.

Consider a Travel Professional

Travel agents not only know which destinations are family friendly, but they often have access to better individual and group rates than you do because of relationships with certain airlines, hotels, and cruise lines. If the airline or hotel of your choice is a partner of your travel agent, or if the agent has suitable alternatives, you can save money for your group.

A travel agent can also provide some protection as well. Should you be bumped from a flight or should your hotel room be substandard, your travel agent's complaint may register more strongly with the airline or hotel and may result in a more satisfactory resolution to your problem.

A good travel agent puts your needs first. Look for an agency that has been in business at least five years, emphasizes customer service, and has someone on staff who specializes in your destination. In addition, make sure the agency belongs to a professional trade organization like the American Society of Travel Agents (ASTA), which maintains a Web site that includes a directory of agents.

Most importantly, the more details you can provide about the kind of trip you're interested in, the better able the travel agent will be to help you.

HOW TO PICK A TRAVEL AGENT

Travel agents are excellent resources. But it's a good idea to collect brochures from several agencies as some agents' suggestions may be influenced by relationships with tour and package firms that reward them for volume sales. If you have a special interest, find an agent with expertise in that area; the American Society of Travel Agents (ASTA) has a database of specialists worldwide.

Make sure your travel agent knows the accommodations and other services of the place being recommended and, preferably, has visited it. Ask about the hotel's location, room size, beds, and whether it has a pool, room service or programs for children, if you care about these.

Do some homework on your own, too. Local tourism boards can provide information about lesser-known and small-niche operators, some of whom may sell only direct to travelers.

All Aboard: Who Is Going?

Before you can begin serious planning, you need to decide which family members will be joining you. First off, does everyone really want to go? If your cousin Al has displayed little interest in the travel plans, he may be telling you something. Trying to persuade him to join the trip may be a disservice to the family.

Are there any tensions among family members that might spoil other people's enjoyment of the trip? If Aunt Gertrude and Aunt Marcy can't put aside their differences at Thanksgiving dinner, the one time of year they meet, it's probably unwise to see if they can work things out on vacation.

Be flexible about allowing outside guests on the trip, but set a limit. You might allow single adult members to bring a companion if they would otherwise be alone among couples. Or the sole child on a trip might bring a friend for company.

Family Needs and Interests

Once you've decided who will go, ask questions of all participants to discover what they want to do and what they consider essential to their comfort. Create a survey, like the one below, asking each person to rank items in importance on a scale of 1 to 5. When you review their answers, you'll have a picture of what matters most to your family.

FAMILY TRAVEL SURVEY

Use a number system to gauge everyone's interest: 5 = strongly prefer; 4 = mildly prefer; 3 = neutral; 2 = mildly against; 1 = strongly against. Count up how many points each criterion gets.

- [ ] A vacation of six days or fewer.
- [ ] A vacation of seven days or more.
- [ ] Stay in one destination.
- [ ] Travel from place to place.
- [ ] Travel in sunny, warm weather.
- [ ] Travel in cool climates.
- [ ] Travel by air.
- [ ] Travel by car.
- [ ] Travel on an independent schedule.
- [ ] Travel on an organized schedule.
- [ ] Good sports and activities facilities.
- [ ] Good food and meal service.
- [ ] Private sleeping room.
- [ ] Travel on a limited budget.
- [ ] Luxury trip.

This is a good time to remind people that some flexibility will be required; it's not possible to accommodate everyone's wishes. Each member of your family will benefit by keeping an open mind.

Special Requirements

In addition to ascertaining family members' general travel requirements and interests, note any individual's special needs in planning for your destination and air and hotel reservations. These might include dietary, medical, or physical concerns. Does anyone require medical facilities near your hotel? A smoke-free or wheelchair-accessible hotel room? Vegetarian or low-cholesterol meals? Special assistance in the airport or a specific seat assignment on the plane? The sooner you gather this information, the easier it will be to find facilities that meet everyone's needs.

Family Planning Meetings

Aunt Mildred calls Pittsburgh home, your parents live in Wichita, and your younger brother Denny roams up and down the West Coast, searching out the best waves. How will you ever manage travel-planning meetings when you're all so scattered? Luckily, telecommunications and the Internet make it easy for families to conduct long-distance meetings. Consider a teleconference or a computer chat room with representatives from other family branches. Or, if all your family members live close by, organize travel-discussion brunches and dinners with the family representatives.

Before you meet for the first time, make sure everyone has completed the travel survey. The goal of the first meeting should be to review what members want to do based on their individual profiles. Find areas of common agreement on major issues: the type of destination, accommodations, and travel. Will this be a visit to a nearby destination, a trip to a different part of the country, or an overseas voyage? Once you've made the general decision—domestic or international, country or city—you and the family representatives can create a list of destination choices. The amount of time and money family members can allot for travel will help you narrow the selection.

A TELECONFERENCE

To organize a telephone conference, contact your long-distance service provider. You'll be referred to a conference organizer who will price the call for you based on the number of participants and the expected duration. Once you determine a time and date, you'll be given a phone number for your family members to call at the appointed hour. When they call in, a phone operator will welcome them to the group and announce that they have joined the call. When everyone is on the line, you can moderate the meeting. If you choose, the call can include a number for people to press on their telephones for the operator to give them their turn as the next speaker. This avoids the confusion of everyone talking at once.

Involving Children in the Planning

Encourage your children to participate and evaluate their choices. If the final destination is not one they voted for, carefully explain the reasoning behind the decision so they know their opinions counted. Once the destination is chosen, involve the children in a more in-depth study of where you are going. Help them write to tourist offices or attractions for brochures. Supervise a Web site search and print and share information about the destination. Look at a map to chart the route. And introduce them to books and videos set in the destination you're visiting.

Zeroing in on a Destination

Once you've eliminated all but a few destinations, allow time for family members to reflect on your short list. There are likely to be two or three good choices; studying the details will lead to the best decision. The deciding factor may be a low airfare or the number of

A CHAT ROOM

A private chat room meeting requires that the participants all have an account with one of the major e-mail providers on the Internet, such as Yahoo or Hotmail. Regardless of your Internet service provider, you can normally sign up with these e-mail companies without paying a fee. If you have a large group of family members with AOL accounts, you can do your e-mail chat on AOL.

family activities. Or it may be special events, such as a festival or historic anniversary, that single out a destination as the best choice.

Resolving Conflicts

The family's collective final decisions may not be the choices you or another family member would make for a personal trip. But remember: the point is to enjoy your family's company in new and pleasant surroundings. Compromise, or even acceptance, when your choices are overlooked is essential. Of course if your hesitation stems from money issues, you may have to graciously decline the trip.

A particular schedule or activity that you consider key to the vacation plans may not appeal to your relatives. Your ideal trip might entail hiking nature trails by day and eating quiet hotel dinners in front of the television at night. Your cousins' plan may be to visit historic sites by day and go club hopping at night. If irreconcilable conflicts emerge in planning, it may be your extended family is not yet ready for a complete vacation together. In this case, separate family-unit trips to a single destination area may be a good option. A reunion of your extended family, even for a day, can be a highlight.

Countdown to Travel

The larger your group, the earlier you'll need to reserve accommodations and transportation. Start a year ahead if you're heading to a popular destination in

A PLANNING TIMELINE

One year ahead
- ☐ Identify participants.
- ☐ Schedule family conferences.
- ☐ Determine budget.
- ☐ Select destination, transportation, lodging.

Eleven months ahead
- ☐ Negotiate hotel, cruise, and air group rates.
- ☐ Communicate rate details to family.

Ten months ahead
- ☐ Book air, cruise, hotel, or lodgings.
- ☐ Leave deposit.
- ☐ Research local activities.
- ☐ Schedule major group functions.
- ☐ Reserve function rooms for family parties.

Six months ahead
- ☐ Make 50% payment. Buy travel insurance.
- ☐ Reserve rental cars or guides.

Five months ahead
- ☐ Let people know that penalties of 25% or more occur for cancellations after this time.
- ☐ Ask participants to gather passports, visas, birth certificates.

high season, such as the Caribbean in winter or if your group numbers 15 or more. For a smaller group, you'll need at least three months to reserve transportation

Three months ahead

- [ ] Make final payment.
- [ ] Select menus for family parties. Advise hosts of special dietary requirements.

One month ahead

- [ ] Full payment lost for any cancellations.
- [ ] Obtain inoculations and medication.
- [ ] Service cars for road trips.
- [ ] Reserve airport transportation.
- [ ] Make restaurant reservations.

Two weeks ahead

- [ ] Reconfirm all arrangements.
- [ ] Confirm special requests with your airline.

One week ahead

- [ ] Make sure every household is ready and has itinerary.
- [ ] Schedule departure-day meeting points and times.
- [ ] Remind everyone to bring travel documents, food and drink.

Day before departure

- [ ] Reconfirm airport-shuttle service. Give arrival times to hotel or rental hosts.

Note that payment and cancellation dates vary by hotel, cruise, and tour company.

and hotel rooms. Adult family members will need this time to arrange for vacation days at work.

A FAMILY REUNION

A family reunion with multiple generations and many branches of the extended family probably means guests will be gathering in one place from all parts of the United States or even other countries. Even if your event involves dozens of family members, there still should be one person in charge. Many resorts insist on dealing with one individual who is responsible for all payments. As when you're planning an extended-family vacation, this person needs experience either planning large business meetings or social gatherings. If you've hosted large parties and know the details of planning vacation travel for your immediate family, you're probably qualified to plan a family reunion. If not, don't despair.

Don't Go It Alone

Resources abound for family-reunion planning. Hotels, cruise ships, and family-vacation resorts have whole departments that specialize in group meetings, including family reunions. Some travel agencies employ group-travel specialists trained to organize meetings. And family-reunion Web sites can connect you to travel professionals, provide reunion planning software, and give you many ideas.

TRACING FAMILY ROOTS

Searching for family roots can be rewarding for a family group traveling to a homeland country or state. About a year ahead of the trip, ask family members to contribute their knowledge of family history. Copies of old photographs with people identified are also helpful. Pool this information and write a collective known history of the family, to distribute at the reunion. Or contact a professional genealogist. The local tourist office for the country you're visiting can help you find tracing services. Historical and genealogical societies can be found in most states and for nearly every nationality. The groups meet and host Internet message boards, where individuals exchange ideas and resources. A few requirements apply in all cases: you'll need original family names, ancestors' first names, and ports of old-country emigration and U.S. immigration. Dates of births, baptisms, marriages, and deaths all can be used to locate entries in government or church registries.

GOING AS A GRANDPARENT

Maybe you're the matriarch of the family, accompanying your children and grandchildren. Or maybe you plan to supervise your grandchildren, without their parents. Whatever the case, a multigenerational-family vacation brings rewards. Sitting around a lodge fire late one snowy night, your children might discover that Grandpa tells a pretty scary story. Your daughter might find that her mother can hold her own at hula lessons. Maybe you'll learn that your 12-year-old grandson is adventurous enough to try escargots on your trip to Paris.

A multigenerational trip also creates challenges. Although your six-year-old granddaughter might be content to ride It's a Small World at Walt Disney World—for three hours a day, every day, on your trip to Orlando—the excitement will quickly wear thin for you. It's important that your trip involve activities that appeal to every generation. And you also need to consider the energy level of all family members. Address these issues early on in the planning stages. You need to ask some important questions before booking travel arrangements.

Physical Challenges

As a grandparent (or travel companion to a grandparent), make an honest evaluation: how much activity do you want? How much are you physically prepared for? Even if keeping up with your grandkids is no problem for a day or weekend, consider how it will feel for a whole vacation. Be prepared for a change in energy level when you head to a hotter, more humid, or colder climate, or to a higher altitude.

Plan rest stops for everyone. At a theme park, for instance, children and parents may become just as tired as grandparents after hours of walking, waiting, and riding. Your family may find the hours at the hotel pool as enjoyable as the time in the parks. Factor physical limitation into your travel plans.

On Walking Trips

Many outdoor destinations that involve walking or hiking provide tour brochures with day-by-day evaluation in their itineraries of the level of physical activity. Make sure that you or the travel planner reads the brochures carefully to establish a few important things.

On a rating scale of one to five what is the activity level each day?

On the same rating scale how steep are the hill climbs each day?

How far will you drive each day?

What are the sightseeing highlights each day?

Where are the best rest stops and meal stops each day?

Where does the journey begin and end?

On Cruises and at Resorts

Cruises and all-inclusive resort properties are ideal for multigenerational trips because they generally provide activities for all ages in a self-contained setting. And with kids' programs, available at most resorts and on most cruises, parents and grandparents can enjoy some time to themselves knowing the children are having fun on their own. On a cruise you might, for example, spend the morning with the kids at the pool and then head off to an adult lecture while the children study sea life with others in their own age group.

Plan Time Alone

Of course you're looking forward to spending time with your children and grandchildren, but you'll enjoy your vacation even more if you plan some time for yourself to rest and recuperate. Schedule, for example, a golf day, a shopping or sightseeing trip, or a night out on the town. If you're staying at a hotel, the concierge can help you plan outings, and the service is free (though you should tip between $5 and $10, more for special services).

Many resort hotels have on-site car-rental desks, where you can conveniently rent a car for a day away from the family. Some car-rental companies will deliver a car to you and return you to your hotel. Others can provide private driver-guides, by advance reservation. Similarly, many one-day-excursion tour companies will pick you up and drop you off. If you can't plan an entire day on your own, even getting away for a morning will provide a nice break.

Who's in Charge?

Before traveling together as grandparents and parents, agree on the level of behavior you expect from the children and discuss the issue of discipline. Avoid having different sets of rules. You may want to sit down together with your children and draw up guidelines beforehand so that everyone's on the same page.

If you're traveling alone with your grandchildren, make sure their parents let the kids know that you'll be in charge in their absence. And it's a good idea to let the kids know that their behavior will determine whether they are mature enough to go on future trips.

Grandparents and Grandchildren Together

If you're taking your grandchildren on vacation without their parents, acquaint yourself with the kids' regular schedules. Although going on vacation necessitates breaking away from everyday activities, children are happier with some semblance of their daily routine. Find out their normal eating and sleeping times, and try to stick to them. If your grandchildren ordinarily sit down to a big breakfast at home, do the same on vacation. If you do stay up late together one night, let them sleep in the next day.

Learn about your grandchildren's likes and dislikes. Does a younger child need a night-light? Do the children like any particular bedtime stories? Do older kids need some time alone? Do any of the kids have strong food preferences? (This is probably not the time to teach them to love broccoli.) You can discover some of these details on your own or by asking the children, but their parents can and should help you avoid surprises.

Before you take and supervise your grandchildren on vacation, ask their parents to prepare them for travel by establishing some rules about bedtimes, rest periods, eating, sharing the TV, playing Gameboy in the car, and activities at the destination. Children need to know that away from their parents, you, the grandparent, are in charge. Talk to the parents about various ways of enforcing rules, such as establishing a penalty system either on the trip or for the return home.

FIRST STEPS WITH
STEPS AND IN-LAWS

You may not be as comfortable traveling with step-relatives and in-laws as you would be with your immediate family, but look on a trip together as an opportunity to discover new things about them. And the reality is that they are a part of your extended family.

If you can't look at it that way, keep in mind that a trip will be better for you and everyone involved if you can all maintain a relaxed, open attitude. You may not get along with your father-in-law, but you married his daughter, and you both want to keep her happy on her dream vacation to Rome. Keep the shortcomings of others to yourself. Remember they're probably making an effort to be positive as well.

TRAVEL LOG

My stepdaughter's college graduation turned out to be a lovely reunion weekend for the far-flung members of our family. The challenge for us was finding a way to minimize the awkward mingling of former spouses and in-laws over the three-day weekend. Her father, grandmother, and I stayed in an all-suite hotel. Her mother and maternal aunt and grandmother stayed in their own suite at a different hotel. Other relatives stayed with friends who lived near campus. My stepdaughter arranged to host a large reception for all family guests in a restaurant with three fellow graduates, and her mom and my husband hosted separate receptions for their sides of the family at their respective hotels. The stage was successfully set for the parents' and grandparents' enjoyment of the larger class celebrations on graduation day, and the smaller, more intimate gatherings were stress-free opportunities for each of us to toast the graduate.

—*Maureen R., Huntington, New York*

First Steps with Steps and In-Laws

The Awkwardness Factor

Major family events like weddings, christenings, graduations, and milestone anniversaries are the most common reasons for a trip throwing step-relatives and in-laws together on the same itinerary. Awkwardness is built-in. A former spouse—the parent of your children—may be meeting your current spouse for the first time. Your parents may be seeing your former in-laws again after a long separation. You may be uncomfortable at first, but don't dwell on it; instead focus on the occasion at hand. Emphasize the event itself. Reacting to the occasion is the best way to alleviate the tension and take the focus off uncomfortable circumstances.

Traveling with a Stepparent

If your cousin Al is bringing his new wife, the stepmother to his children, make a special effort to make her feel welcome. Traveling for the first time in the role of surrogate mother (or father) is tough enough; it's even harder knowing that your new extended family is comparing you to the children's birth mother. By embracing the new wife as a member of your family, you help the children learn to accept their new stepmother as well.

If you're a new stepparent traveling with your stepchildren and spouse for the first time, sit down as a family and talk about what to expect on this trip. You'll want to discuss discipline beforehand with your

EX-SPOUSES AND YOUR CHILDREN'S NEEDS

When traveling with your children, consult with your former spouse about the travel planning so the children know both of you are in agreement. Together, create a travel checklist for the children's needs.

- [ ] Set a schedule. Agree when the children will leave home and return.

- [ ] Agree on who will be traveling with the children. No surprise guests.

- [ ] Give contact information on your day-by-day itinerary. Get contact information for the nontraveling spouse.

- [ ] Agree on how much money the ex-spouse will give the children to travel and how they may spend it.

- [ ] Agree with ex-spouse on any activities (skiing, hiking, sightseeing, swimming). Secure approval for any risky activities such as horseback riding, parasailing, and diving.

- [ ] Agree generally on what the children will and will not be eating.

spouse. Also be aware of any issues your spouse and ex-husband or ex-wife have expressed about the children's activities on this trip.

Traveling with Parents-in-Law

Talk openly with your in-laws about any awkward situations that arise during both planning and travel. Keep things positive and avoid putting your spouse in the middle of every communication. Be as diplomatic as possible and pay particular attention to your in-laws' suggestions. Keep in mind that you and your spouse will have opportunities to travel alone in the future.

Vacation Rehearsal

If you haven't spent a lot of time with your in-laws apart from the occasional family dinner, consider a short excursion before embarking on a big trip together. Spend a day together at a ball game or go sightseeing in the nearest big city. In the evening, try dinner and a show to see how everyone interacts. Be sure to make travel a topic of conversation. Where have your in-laws traveled and where did they stay? What did they like and dislike? Share your own experiences and preferences. If you sense that you're not yet ready for a trip together, get to know more about each other and leave open the option of future family trips.

TRAVELING IN A
NONTRADITIONAL FAMILY

Whether you're a single parent, part of a same-sex couple, or a parent with children from different unions, anticipate and address beforehand any problems you might encounter during your trip.

Perhaps you're a parent with teenagers from a first marriage and young children with a current spouse or partner. When looking for a destination, you need to balance the needs of your teenage children with those of your younger children. A cruise with an assortment of onboard activities, for example, is a good choice. Some cruise ships have children's programs for each of several age groups. Just remember: if the destination you choose doesn't hold some appeal for all of your kids, you'll probably hear about it.

Don't assume your older kids want to baby-sit for your toddlers. If you do ask an older child to do one or two nights of child-care duty, say so before you leave and arrange for some small reward. Otherwise, check beforehand to make sure that baby-sitting services are available at your destination if you plan on a parents' night out.

PROCLAIM YOUR IDENTITY

For the ultimate in kitschy fun, have special T-shirts printed up for your gang. Have one of the most creative among you come up with a slogan and a design, then use iron-on transfers to customize inexpensive solid-color T-shirts. If you are traveling to a theme park or getting together in a park or other crowded place, choose a bright color as the base—it will make it easier for you to keep track of each other. If you have many T-shirts to print, you can have it professionally done. The tab can be built into the overall price of each household's travel arrangements, or you can all pay separately.

If you're a member of a same-sex couple and you're not the one doing the planning, for example, steer the travel planner away from destinations you know have less-than-tolerant attitudes.

BENEFIT FROM THE UNEXPECTED

Who knows what unexpected events will transpire to help shape your family vacation. Go with the flow. Your 12-year-old may come up with a great idea for a trip that everyone else overlooked. A friend may have a fabulous vacation rental at just the right time. A travel sale or special promotion may come along that makes the trip more affordable. A wedding engagement or other special event may bring more family members into the trip. Whatever happens, make the most of it—and consider each new positive development a sign that your family vacation is meant to be.

The Travel Budget

IDEAS FOR YOUR DREAM FAMILY GATHERING flow fast and furious from your excited family members. But sooner or later the vacation will have to be paid for.

Be comprehensive in your calculations of how much the trip will cost each household. In your early planning meetings, agree with family leaders that before booking any travel you will break down and evaluate the costs of each vacation plan. Arrive at a mutually agreed upon price per adult and per child. Include costs of long distance and local transportation, lodging, meals, beverages, entertainment, gratuities, special events, and sports activities.

If you can agree on a group budget per person for transportation and lodging, you can negotiate a better deal for all than if people make personal arrangements. No doubt the more affordable you can make the trip, the more family members will be able to join you.

To estimate incidental costs in a particular destination, obtain a current destination guidebook and call the city, state, or country tourist office among others, to get the details. How much is a local taxi ride, a beer or a cappuccino, an orchestra concert ticket, a museum entrance, a three-day bus pass? Ask for the cost of incidentals at the hotel you've chosen. Think of other everyday items your family may want to purchase. Distribute a list of these local costs to your relatives, along with your estimated per-person travel costs.

REACHING A **COMFORT LEVEL**

Your family will enjoy the vacation much more if everyone is comfortable with the cost. If you can't agree on a budget within the means of each family member, you may see people dropping out of the trip. Or perhaps family members will agree to a trip costing more than they can comfortably afford, only to grow resentful during the vacation. And a bill-paying hangover could make them less likely to join in future family vacations.

FINDING DEALS

If getting the best possible price on your trip is a priority, start scouring the travel sections of newspapers both in your own area and in your destination. Local newspapers from your potential travel destinations usually have more and deeper discounts in both their travel and classified ad sections than your newspapers back home. Try to obtain these papers for your planning via a news service or through the mail; many major papers have Web sites you can access free of charge, and the sites often include the travel and classified sections. For example, you can find budgetwise cruise offers in south Florida newspapers because many ships are homeported in Miami and Fort Lauderdale for part of the year. London's newspapers are good for travel deals within Great Britain and on the Continent. In addition, try an on-line search. For example, almost every major airline now offers lower fares when you purchase tickets through their Web sites. And you can find other good deals on travel Web sites such as Expedia, Orbitz, CheapTickets, and Travelocity.

All designated family contacts should weigh in at a budget discussion. Try to make the experience a positive one. As planner, you'll need to create agreement on what constitutes affordable travel and then be sensitive to excessive or unnecessary travel expenditures. Expect and allow for different families' budgets. Uncle Phil and Aunt June may opt to upgrade to first-class airfare and suite accommodations. Your brother may decide he and his wife want their children in the same room while your cousins prefer to pay for a separate room for their kids. Building in some flexibility is a good idea. Remember this trip is about family rather than frills.

Measuring Family Means

Most people want to keep their personal finances private. You may have an idea of relatives' means based on profession, residence, car, and other clues, but their credit card debt, monthly living expenses, education costs, and other financial details may be invisible to you. In addition, people prioritize how they spend their money differently.

Yet there are tactful ways to learn how much a particular family group can afford or is willing to pay.

Ask family groups from the start what they consider to be a reasonable price tag for a vacation. Determine how long their last vacation was, what kind of hotel they stayed in, and whether they flew or drove. Do they think they received good value or overpaid for the trip? Find out if the household prefers to dine out, eat in, or order takeout, and what types of meals it prefers. Does this group rent a car on vacation, drive its own, or do without a car? Does the group use public city transportation or use taxis? Learn whether the household needs all the comforts of home while traveling or prefers a simpler travel lifestyle. Gathering this information will give you clues on how much family groups are willing to pay for food, transportation, and other details that will figure into your travel budget.

Accommodating Different Budgets

Your siblings, aunts, uncles, parents, grandparents, and in-laws may be spread across a variety of professions and income brackets, at different stages in their careers and savings. To bring everyone together on one trip, you'll likely have to bring the trip down to a level acceptable to the lowest income earners: you're most likely to successfully bring everyone together if you can plan travel on a budget that accommodates family members with less money to spend.

Broach the subject first with the individuals or couples you know to be the most affluent. Without singling out specific family members who may have less discretionary income, discuss your concerns and expectation that a less expensive trip will probably work best for your family. You might even suggest your own budget would be stretched by an expensive trip. Make sure your more affluent relatives do not influence other members to agree to a trip beyond their means.

The Luxury Travelers

If you (or other relatives) are accustomed to luxury trips, you have to make a choice. You can accept a less extravagant trip than you'd normally take, staying in the same place and eating the same food as your relatives. Or you can upgrade to more expensive accommodations nearby. If you want to stay close to the rest of your family, you might stay with them in the same location but choose a balcony room or even a suite in a hotel or on a cruise ship. Or maybe you'll fly or rent a car while other members drive their family car to save money. Whatever your arrangements, make sure that family members are comfortable with a plan that may not have equal components for all.

Lending a Hand to In-Laws

It's often awkward for a financially strapped young family to accept financial support from wealthier parents (or grandparents or other relatives) to join a trip. Although this may be acceptable to the child, it can be uncomfortable for the spouse—the daughter- or son-in-law. If you are the parent in this situation, speak to your child about ways of making his or her spouse comfortable with accepting financial help, and then speak directly to your son- or daughter-in-law. Consider a compromise in which you pay, perhaps, for your grandchildren while your child and spouse pay their own way. If resolution of the issue seems unlikely, don't force the subject. Do whatever possible to prevent any serious division between your son or daughter and spouse over the question of accepting your money to help them travel.

More affluent family members can also diplomatically help pay a larger share by offering their frequent flier miles to relatives, agreeing to pay vacation costs on a prorated basis determined by household income, or agreeing to bring all the extras such as food, beverages, or other travel necessities.

Affordability Equals Happiness

The best vacation happens when everyone can concentrate on having fun. Sure, your trip can be luxurious if a more expensive resort is within everyone's budget. But the point, after all, is to spend time with your family, enjoying their company.

ESTIMATE AT-HOME EXPENSES

When deciding how much you can afford to spend on your family vacation, consider:

- [ ] What is your monthly discretionary income?
- [ ] Do you have major nontravel expenses ahead: taxes, home improvement, auto repairs, or medical bills?
- [ ] Are you carrying high credit card debt?
- [ ] Are there expenses you can postpone?
- [ ] Are back-to-school expenses looming?

Children Don't Worry

If the kids in your family think there's no finer meal than peanut-butter-and-jelly sandwiches and chocolate milk, chances are they won't be too concerned about where they eat. In fact, most kids prefer cheaper eats and hotels that don't class children in the same category as vermin. Their main concern is mostly whether there are other children and a pool. Keep that in mind as you consider accommodations.

All the children should have equal access to recreation, water activities, family parties, and treats.

FAMILY BUDGET PLANNER

Transportation

Home-airport transfers (round-trip)	$_____
Airfare (round-trip)	$_____
Hotel-airport transfers (round-trip)	$_____
Car transportation	
Rental (with taxes and options)	$_____
Family car (maintenance)	$_____
Fuel and tolls	$_____
Taxis	$_____
Train or bus ticket (round-trip)	$_____
Tips (round-trip)	$_____
Subtotal	$_____

Accommodations

Daily base hotel or rental rate x days	$_____
Taxes	$_____
Tips	$_____
Subtotal	$_____

Meals

Breakfast × days	$_____
Lunch × days	$_____
Dinner × days	$_____
Snacks	$_____
Subtotal	$_____

Entertainment

Sports fees and rentals	$_____
Spa treatments	$_____
Show or concert tickets	$_____
Admission fees	$_____
Guided tours	$_____
Club cover charges	$_____
Drinks	$_____
Airport snacks, drinks on plane	$_____
Airplane headsets	$_____
Subtotal	$_____

Special Family Events
Room rentals $____
Meals (include snack foods) $____
Bar costs $____
Entertainment/music charges $____
Tips and service charges $____
Subtotal $_____

Extras
Shopping $____
Passports and visas $____
Trip insurance $____
Immunizations $____
Miscellaneous (film, sunscreen, etc.) $____
ATM charges $____
Subtotal $_____

Contingency—Just in Case
                                              $_____

TOTAL $_____

Divide by the number of vacation days to get the price per person per day. Costs such as car rentals, family car, or transfers are priced per household. Divide these costs by persons in the household to determine the per-person cost for each item.

Play It Again

Another good reason for moderate spending? You may like your extended-family vacation so much, you'll want to repeat the gathering next year. If all the family households have stayed within their budgets, there's a good chance that everyone will want to go again.

Turn on Your Calculator

Approach your family's travel budget with the attention to detail you would use in calculating your expense report after a business trip.

The first cost area to consider is transportation to and from the destination, and the second is per day living costs per adult or per child once you get there. While you may be eating light or casual meals on certain days, and splurging at expensive restaurants on others, you can calculate an expected average cost of food per person per day. Incidental costs, such as gifts or drinks not consumed at family meals or parties, should be at the discretion of each individual.

Ready, Set, Shop

Many travelers consider bargain hunting their number one vacation activity. Your vacation destination may have discount outlets or jewelry or leather centers where the cost of shopping is cheaper than at home. Or the region might be known for a typical craft. And since your guard is down on vacation, you're probably less reticent about whipping out the credit card to make purchases. Remind everyone to budget for shopping and souvenirs.

PUTTING TOGETHER **THE TRIP**

Once everyone agrees to pay an equal share per person, or per accommodation, you can more easily negotiate a group rate. For 15 or more guests, contact the group sales department of the hotel, resort, or cruise line.

Getting the Most for Your Money

Remember buying your last car? You researched, visited several dealers—even for the same model car—kicked the tires, and sought out the best bargain. Buy family travel in the same way: study, negotiate, and compare options with different travel companies, even for the same vacation choice, to get your best deal. This is when you should draw on the talents of your most convincing family negotiator and your best financial manager.

Travel Agents and Travel Dollars

Ask about package deals, comparing the value benefits of the package to buying travel components separately. Take notes on features and pricing and check directly with the hotel to see if it has a better deal of its own. If your agent simply hands you travel brochures and has little to say, you have the wrong person and should find someone better. List all the services the travel agent promises or guarantees, in case anything goes wrong with the travel company or arrangements before or during your trip. Get everything in writing.

Most agents now charge a consulting fee. The fee, which pays for the agent's time, should be applied to the price of your vacation if you decide to book with the agent.

Negotiating Group Rates

Agree on a range of room rates you are authorized to seek on behalf of the extended family. Your goal is to negotiate a price well below published brochure rates.

HOW TO GET GREAT RATES: QUESTIONS TO EXPLORE

- ☐ Are you traveling off-season? Can you?
- ☐ Will you purchase group meals, which might allow for a greater room discount?
- ☐ Are promotional rates available at a lower cost than your group rate?
- ☐ Does a family member have frequent guest or flier points for discounts or free nights?
- ☐ Will the hotel give you a discount for paying by check instead of credit card?
- ☐ Can your first hotel choice match lower rates offered by competing nearby hotels?
- ☐ Can you negotiate extras: a free reception, an extra night's stay, or a sports-activity package?

Start by asking the hotel's group sales manager for a rate well below the absolute highest amount you are willing to pay per person or per room; chances are you'll have to negotiate up to a higher rate.

Group Benefits on Cruises

You have some onboard buying power based on the size of your group, so take advantage of it. Negotiate with the group sales department of your cruise line or have your travel agent negotiate for perks when booking your ship. With so many more new ships and more competition than ever before, you should be able to select three or four ships from different lines and negotiate your best deal. Let each line know you're negotiating with the competition, and have each group sales department provide a written offer. A good travel agent can help you, but be wary if your travel agent works closely with one line for a commission.

If you bring an extended-family group that requires at least 15 cabins or more to a ship (fewer when lines are discounting a cruise), your minimum discount should be one free cabin for the group. If you can't get a free cabin, ask for other discounts, such as shipboard credit or free parties.

A cruise line generally expects a large group will spend money on wine, merchandise, and other extras. And now most lines offer a group amenity package with benefits ranging from shipboard credits and free shore guides to a private cocktail party. If you have a group of 50 or more, some cruise lines throw in a cocktail party with free drinks and hors d'oeuvres. Insist on this. Inspect the shipboard room for your reception when you get on board; if you're not thrilled, ask for something nicer. The line wants your repeat business and will do everything possible to make your cruise experience a positive one.

Paying to Play

Ask each family household for a 10% to 15% deposit to secure guest rooms, vacation rentals, or ship staterooms. The deposit commits them to the trip. Most hospitality properties won't take a reservation without the deposit. Generally, members of your group need to pay half their room amount for the whole trip by about six months before arrival, with the final payment due about three months ahead. In most cases, the closer you book to your travel dates, the larger the deposit required. If you book less than three months ahead, you may have to pay in full to secure reservations.

Travel Insurance

Invest in a comprehensive travel-insurance policy that includes coverage for your family group for trip cancellation and interruption, default, trip delay, and medical expenses.

Without insurance you will lose all or most of your money if you cancel your trip, regardless of the reason.

Default insurance covers you if your tour operator, airline, or cruise line goes out of the business. Trip-delay covers expenses that arise because of bad weather or mechanical delays. Study the fine print when comparing policies.

Always buy travel policies directly from the insurance company; if you buy them from a cruise line, airline, or tour operator that goes out of business, you probably will not be covered for the agency or operator's default, a major risk. Before making any purchase, have family members review their existing health and homeowner's policies to find out what they cover away from home.

Reviving the Dropouts

Set strict payment deadlines and let members know ahead of time that missing them either jeopardizes your group rate or forces the family to invite other guests to replace late payers. Your chances of having a family member with a payment problem or a need to drop out of the trip increase with the size of your group. If a family member runs into financial problems before the trip, he or she may decide to opt out of traveling if there is no penalty or rate increase. Or the family as a whole might decide to cover the missing payment to save a group rate from increasing or to keep the member from dropping out. Another option is to invite additional relatives or close family friends as replacements. Discuss this with the family before inviting outsiders to join the trip.

Using E-Mail

Keep an e-mail address book on your computer with the home or office e-mail address for every family-group representative (or someone in each family group, if the representative doesn't have e-mail). As you make payments, develop itineraries, and receive receipts, you can instantly transmit the news to everyone with one group message. The e-mail broadcast enables all the members to respond to you and each other.

BACK UP YOUR RECORDS

A computer is great for keeping records, but there's always a risk, no matter how small, that a glitch will cause you to lose an important file or message. In addition to all of your electronic documents, keep a notebook with important phone numbers and information. Put all paper correspondence—receipts, records, printed versions of important e-mail messages—into this book, and keep it with your other travel-planning information. This keeps records in one place, makes them easier to find and carry with you, and gives you a backup in case of a computer mishap.

Fare and Rate Changes

Take advantage of promotions and travel sales, even after you've made reservations. When you reserve group airfare or individual fares, find out what your options are in case the fare drops. You may be able to receive credit back for the value of the price reduction. In the case of an airfare reduction, you might have to pay a handling charge of up to $75 per person for re-ticketing, but the fee could be worth it if the fare difference is substantial. In a hotel-room-rate reduction, your best bet is to request that you receive a credit on your credit card to be used toward the family's purchase of meals, activities, or other extras.

Handling the Money

Keep careful records, either on your computer (with additional printed versions) or in your notebook, when it comes to handling family members' money. If you've designated a family banker to do this, you might still want to keep backup versions for your own records. Account for every family member's payment at the time you receive it. Note in duplicate—one copy for you and one for the payer—the amount of money you received and the method of payment. You might want to open a separate, interest-bearing bank account in which to deposit funds until you need to forward them to travel suppliers. Use the same record keeping to note payments made to travel companies. Confirm each one with a receipt.

Personal Finance Software

A personal finance software program for your home computer like Quicken or Microsoft Money helps manage your family travel budget and can help you track expenses. Be sure to opt for products focused on personal budget management and not those detailing financial market investments or tax strategies.

No Surprises

Everyone in the family should agree from the start to share any financial information that affects payment for the trip. If someone has a financial obstacle that delays his or her payment or may prevent him or her from going, the group needs to know. A dropout may require others to pay more money or may inspire relatives to offer help.

If you, as the planner, encounter unforeseen surcharges, price disagreements, or other conflicts with the travel hosts, share these with the family if the problems can't be quickly resolved. Your family needs to be prepared for price increases, and it's possible someone in your family may be able to help you deal with unforeseen money problems. You also want everyone to know that the problem is not of your making.

An Easy Payment Plan

For each stage of payment you make to travel suppliers, be sure family members have submitted payments to you before you lay out any large sum, especially cash. Have your relatives pay you first by check or cash before you hand over your own credit card information to the airline or hotel.

Always record each family member's payment and make sure the record includes your copy of the receipt. This may sound overly business-like and formal, but with so many people giving you money at different times, it's easy to lose track. Records are the best way to protect your family's money and your own goodwill as the family travel planner.

Reading the Mouse Print

The back or inside cover of most travel brochures normally includes a full page or two of small type under the headline "Terms and Conditions" or "General

THE USUAL CONDITIONS IN BROCHURES

- ☐ Deposit and final-payment dates.
- ☐ Credit cards accepted.
- ☐ Items included and not included in each person's price.
- ☐ Cancellation penalties based on dates.
- ☐ Any order processing and change fees.
- ☐ Gratuity policies.
- ☐ Policy in case your travel host has to change or substitute arrangements.
- ☐ Trip protection insurance options.

Information." If you do not have a brochure and are staying at a resort, ask the property to send you a copy of their terms. Make copies of this information (you may want to enlarge the type on a copy machine) and send a copy to each household traveling with your extended family. Highlight in yellow some of the most important items. Inform everyone in the family of what is required of them on each point, such as how much they are expected to tip people who serve them.

A Banker and Cash Pool

Sharing out-of-pocket travel expenses can be a thorny issue during group trips. These include gas, tolls, meals at roadside stops or in airports, and tips for hotel porters and others. Consider appointing a "banker" to handle these payments. Try to estimate the costs of extras ahead of time, and prepare your family to contribute money to a cash pool. At the start of the trip, each household contributes its fair share—say $25 per day to start, more if there are children. The banker then draws on the pool to pay for extra expenses until the cash is exhausted. Then start over again with more money. Although the division of funds may not come out exactly to the dollar for each group, the pool idea will save you a lot of time.

Handling Travel Complaints

Many travel companies include their complaint and refund policy in their written terms and conditions. Obtain a copy of the policy or learn about it before you buy the trip.

Complaints within a group can often be personal. Your room may be fine, but your Aunt Mildred's may not, based on her view, an insect problem, or her personal perception of size or service. Agree among your family members before the trip that if someone is unhappy, you and the offended traveler can try to get a better arrangement from your host. Request a response immediately during the trip and document all information. It may not be possible to fix the problem on the spot. A ship may not be able to find you a new cabin, or a hotel may not have any other free rooms.

If your complaint is not resolved, file a claim for a refund when you get home using forms provided by the cruise line, resort company, or tour operator, making sure that all your complaints have been documented with managers' names and receipts.

If you've used a travel agent, he or she should help, even while you are on the trip. Often a travel agent's complaint will register more strongly with the airline or hotel manager. American Express Platinum card and Diners Club card representatives, whom you can contact by a phone number on your card, can also step in and lobby on your behalf during your trip.

If the situation cannot be resolved immediately, don't let it ruin your trip. Make the best of the situation, perhaps by arranging for a special treat for your disgruntled relative—perhaps a night out at the restaurant of his or her choice. And if another family member doesn't mind a smaller room or a view of another building, perhaps he or she could switch rooms with Aunt Mildred.

IDENTIFYING HIDDEN COSTS

Before you commit to a trip to a desired destination with an attractive price, check the fine print. Learn what's included in and what's missing from the headline price. There are obvious considerations: is the hotel rate per person or per room? Is airfare one-way or round-trip? Are meals included or extra? Look also for hidden costs: how much are taxes? Are there airport surcharges? Does a vacation rental rate exclude extra charges such as maid service? Identifying hidden costs will help you determine the true price of the trip and will save your family from unforeseen travel expenses.

All-Inclusives and Noninclusives

The term "all-inclusive," usually used in connection with a resort, is loosely interpreted in the travel industry. Most of the time, the term applies to resorts where you don't have to dip into your pocket each day to pay for food, drink, and activities. But some properties, deceptively, work in extra charges. So if you're considering an all-inclusive resort vacation for your family, identify exactly what's included. Some resorts include wine or other drinks with meals, but not between meals or during evening entertainment. Some charge extra to use water-sports equipment.

DECEPTIVE PRICES

Study consumer-travel advertising in newspapers, magazines, and Web sites before you make purchases for your extended-family vacation. Many price headlines in travel ads use the term "from" followed by a price, as in "From $1,000." This is the lead price and may apply to only one or two undesirable hotels, neither in an ideal location. When you check with the advertiser, you may find the hotel that interests you charges much more than the advertised rate. The same is true of hotel rates that look good—but are per person rather than per room. Also be wary of rates that look attractive but require a minimum number of nights.

With a true all-inclusive program you have a fairly accurate picture of the price of your vacation in advance. If you want to play sports activities every day, or plan to celebrate with drinks and hotel entertainment most nights, you definitely save on the all-inclusive compared to paying as you go. A noninclusive program gives you the freedom to plan each vacation day as it comes. You are not financially tied to the activities and

WHAT'S NOT INCLUDED?

Many all-inclusive resorts don't include equipment for motorized water sports like waterskiing, jet skiing, and parasailing because of the extra costs of fuel, insurance, and guides. If these water sports are important to your family, look for the word "motorized" when selecting water sports as part of a resort package. Otherwise you may have to arrange them through an outside outfitter. Water-sports equipment you can expect from your all-inclusive beach resort includes surf or boogie boards, inner tubes, rubber rafts, life jackets, snorkeling gear, and perhaps equipment for team sports such as water polo.

Inclusive entertainment usually means after-dinner musical performances or dancing at the hotel's nightclub. Find out ahead of time whether your all-inclusive resort includes drinks in the club as part of your package.

dining facilities in the hotel, allowing you to explore other options without feeling as if you've already paid for them.

If most family members don't plan on drinking or making use of the extras of an all-inclusive package, à la carte is the way to go. In this situation, look for hotels that let you choose between all-inclusive and noninclusive plans, a great option when members of your family can't agree on the issue. Your all-inclusive guests will be given a hotel card or wristband that pays for all included meals and activities. Your noninclusive guests can participate but they'll pay as they go.

Get every promise that matters to you in writing, and be sure to bring the letter along with you on the trip in case a promised benefit is missing.

Cruises: Not Really All-Inclusive

The price you pay for a cruise cannot be considered all-inclusive. Beverages, both alcoholic and nonalcoholic, are charged by the drink, and an automatic gratuity of 15% is added to your bill. All ship-operated shore excursion tours are extra, as are spa treatments, the rental of beach equipment, onboard video games, laundering and dry cleaning, and the use of e-mail or the Internet at onboard computers. Some, but not all, ships may charge you an hourly fee for baby-sitting, and some ships add an automatic gratuity per passenger on your bill at the end of the cruise for tips to the crew.

Once upon a time, cruises included all meals in the price, and you were seated at the same dinner table at a scheduled time with the same waiters and guests each night. Now, on some lines, you'll find smaller, more numerous dining areas known as "restaurants at sea." Because guests eat at different dining areas each night and because the quality of food varies from restaurant to restaurant, you must often pay a surcharge—usually anywhere from $5 to $20 extra per meal.

Check with your cruise line or travel agent before booking to determine what is and isn't included in your cruise. Make a list of all possible extras and figure out ahead of the trip how much these will cost.

Maid Service

If you choose a vacation rental or a resort with kitchen facilities but no daily maid service, consider hiring help. Kitchen facilities are a great way to save money, but you and other family members may not want to be burdened with cooking every meal for a large group. And keeping the place clean with so many people around may be a problem. The cost of hiring help may seem reasonable once you divvy up the fee among family members.

Most rental communities have an in-house rental manager who can provide information on hiring help. The local tourist office may also have suggestions.

A GOOD DEAL OR A BAD ONE?

Remember the too-good-to-be-true rule: if the cost sounds so generous it can't possibly be true, it probably isn't. Be skeptical if someone promises you an all-inclusive vacation to a beautiful destination at a rock-bottom price. Check every detail carefully—be sure to read the fine print—and back away if the sales agent evades your questions. Don't send money until your doubts and concerns have been properly addressed and you have proof of what you're getting for the money you're paying.

Make sure you obtain and check past client references before considering any hire.

If someone in your family has a cook or housekeeper, he or she might be invited to come along to help out. The cost of airfare and accommodations may be well worth the money.

Taxes, Service Charges, Extras

Hidden hotel and car-rental charges can quickly raise the base price of your family vacation. That great car-rental rate you've been quoted can quickly grow once you factor in mileage charges, insurance, taxes, and other extras. Some hotels, including those on small Caribbean islands, in Mexican resort towns, and in some U.S. cities, apply mandatory hotel-bed taxes, per person, to help pay for local tourism promotion. Fees to use hotel room telephones, even if you use your own credit or calling card for long-distance service, can be as high as $1.50 or more per call. Some resorts charge a maintenance fee, and some vacation homeowners a cleaning fee. Get these extra costs in writing ahead of time.

Prearranged Tours and Packages

Because everything is packaged by professionals, you spend less time planning—and often get it all at a good price. Still the level of inclusiveness varies from one package to the next. Remember that the more your package or tour includes the better you can predict the ultimate cost of your vacation. Make sure you know exactly what is covered, and beware of hidden costs. Are taxes, tips, and transfers included? Entertainment and excursions? These can add up.

Caution

Each year consumers are stranded or lose their money when tour operators—even large ones with excellent reputations—go out of business. So check the operator. Ask several travel agents about its reputation and try to book with a company that has a consumer protection program (look for information in the company's brochure). In the United States, your money is protected if you book with members of the National Tour Association and the U.S. Tour Operators Association, which have special programs to cover your payments and travel arrangements in the event the company defaults. It's also a good idea to choose a company that participates in the American Society of Travel Agents' Tour Operator Program (TOP). ASTA will act as a mediator in any disputes between you and your TOP-member tour operator.

THE FAMILY ANGEL

Maybe a gift is making this extended-family vacation possible. Perhaps you're a grandparent who wants to treat your grandchildren to a trip. Or maybe you want to help siblings who would otherwise be unable to afford this vacation. Maybe your parents are offering to pay your way on the trip. Whatever the situation, be aware that as wonderful and generous as a travel gift may be, there may be some awkwardness attached to the situation. Money is, after all, a sensitive issue, perhaps even more so when it's between family members and when it involves a large sum required for a vacation.

If you're the benefactor, one of the best ways to overcome any awkwardness is to find a special reason for your gift. Turn it into an anniversary, birthday, graduation, or holiday present. Many travel companies even have gift certificates that can put pretty packaging on your travel gift.

Remember, for this to be a truly enjoyable family vacation, offer or accept a trip without a hidden agenda.

When Your Relative Pays

Lucky you! Someone wants to give you the gift of travel. If a relative, in good faith, wants to help you financially on this trip, accept with class and dignity. Express thanks and show your gratitude—either with a gift or special dinner.

If Strings Are Attached

When you accept paid travel from your parents, brothers, sisters, or adult children, make sure there are no unwelcome expectations of you, either during or after the trip. Is your uncle paying your way because he wants you to baby-sit during the trip? Are your parents paying because they want to see more of their grandchildren and expect more visiting from you after the trip is over? Are your adult children paying for you to see your grandchildren on vacation because they have other plans for Thanksgiving, when you would really like to see the kids?

Everyone will benefit from an honest and open discussion of what to expect. But try to be as tactful as possible. Decide if it's worth it to you to fulfill certain expectations to go on this trip.

Preferential Treatment

All family members should play a role in planning your family vacation. But when a relative pays for you or your children, he or she should have extra input in choosing the destination and planning the itinerary. Let the food, schedule, or the entertainment be closer to his or her tastes than yours for at least part of the vacation.

This does not mean, however, that your relative should rule this vacation with an iron fist, especially if you and your family have been planning this trip from the beginning as a family vacation. It will hardly be enjoyable if only one or two people make crucial decisions for the rest of your group. If a family benefactor initiates the vacation with the idea of going to a particular destination, then you'll likely have to bow to his or her wishes, or decide if it's worth it to you to go on the trip.

What the Kids Know

When discussing travel plans with children who are of school age, keep things honest and open. If this trip is Grandma's or Uncle Al's treat, the children should know so they can say thanks. It may also be important to the benefactor that kids know what Grandma or Uncle Al has done for them.

Expressing Gratitude

Find creative ways to show thanks, both during and after the trip, to your generous relatives.

Make sure your family angels have the best room.

Send flowers or champagne to their room with a thank-you card.

Plan a special dinner with a customized cake.

Arrange for an evening out, complete with driver, dinner, and a show.

You can also express thanks with an event at home a month or two after the trip. If a holiday is approaching, make it a holiday party. Develop the film and make it a picture swap—or give an album as a gift. If you have a date in mind, hand out invitations to everyone at the vacation farewell dinner. Make sure the date is flexible in case your guests of honor or any other family members are busy.

Thanks from the Kids

Have your children express their appreciation to grandparents, aunts, and uncles who have made their vacation possible. During the trip, video the children having fun and saying thanks on camera. Have the kids serve their grandparents breakfast in bed one morning with the help of room service staff. Collect seashells and create a picture frame for their travel photo. Let the children select some favorite pictures of themselves with their relatives on the trip; create a photo album and give it to the benefactors along with the children's handmade thank-you card.

Places to Go, Things to Do

YOUR EXTENDED FAMILY IS REVVED UP for a vacation together. You've determined who's going, and you've set a rough budget. You also have a good idea of when you can travel. Now comes the best part: deciding where to go. Use your imagination, and let the decision-making process with your family be fun. Even if you're planning on a budget with limited time, you have a wealth of destinations to choose from. Just because you're staying within the continental United States doesn't mean that trip can't be as exciting, fun-packed, and novel as a voyage to another country.

WHAT KIND OF DESTINATION?

Your family's original travel survey will help determine where you should go. If no one wants to fly, then your destinations will be governed by how far you're willing to drive or take a train or bus. If only one person insists on warm weather, the Caribbean won't be on your short list.

Before you start discussing places, you first need to figure out what *kind* of destination everyone is most interested in—big city, beach, countryside. Once you have a handle on this, then you can zero in on your family's dream trip.

Comparing Surveys

There are two questionnaires in this book—not to make things more complicated but to help you narrow your choices. The first one in Chapter 1 addresses the brass tacks of the vacation, such as length of time, distance people are willing to travel, and the level of luxury they expect. The second survey deals with locations and what those locations will provide. Look at both surveys together and you should have a pretty

WHAT APPEALS TO YOU?

Use a number system to gauge everyone's interest: 5 = strongly prefer; 4 = mildly prefer; 3 = neutral; 2 = mildly against; 1 = strongly against. Count up how many points each choice gets.

- ☐ Lots of activities.
- ☐ Lots of relaxing.
- ☐ Participation sports involved.
- ☐ Nature and outdoor activities.
- ☐ Selection of quality restaurants.
- ☐ Cultural activities available.
- ☐ Good nightlife options.
- ☐ Plenty of shopping.
- ☐ Beach or resort with little sightseeing.
- ☐ Beach or resort with sightseeing options.
- ☐ Big city.
- ☐ Touring place to place.
- ☐ Staying in one place.
- ☐ Variety shows.
- ☐ Roller coasters or other rides.
- ☐ Cruise.
- ☐ Camping or hiking.
- ☐ Skiing.

good picture of where everyone's mind is. The world is a big place filled with potential vacation spots, so evaluating both surveys will help to eliminate whole areas, hopefully reducing the time you have to spend on your research.

WHAT'S YOUR TRAVEL STYLE?

There's no doubt that every family has its own vacation style, even though few families are aware of it. Some go all out on their vacations, even if they live more conservatively the rest of the year. Some people wouldn't be caught dead sleeping in a tent, even though they like to go on day hikes at home. Even in one immediate family, there can be different approaches: Your son likes to sleep late, while his sister is waiting for the pool to open at 9 AM. You want to hit all the art galleries, while your spouse would rather hang out in a café. Your parents may just want to get some sun and read a book. Coordinating one family is tough; gauging the whole clan is an even bigger challenge. The exciting part is that many destinations offer something for everyone. Identifying the different styles and understanding what the destinations have to offer is the goal.

Have each family's point person make the assessment and relay the information to the planner.

Go-Goers

Waking at the crack of dawn, going all day, resting for an hour and heading back out again may sound exhausting, but some people are completely invigorated by the up and at 'em attitude. You've saved for this trip and spent a lot of time planning it, so you want to get the most out of the destination. Sound completely reasonable? Then you're a go-goer. Look for destinations where there are a lot of activities for daytime and enough to do at night.

Consider: Big cities, resorts with sports facilities, theme parks.

Culture Vultures

If you don't mind going to the movies on a beautiful, sunny day, you just might be a culture vulture. Is the first thing you want to know about a city, "Which way to the museum?" or "Where can I buy the gallery guide?" Do you spend four hours walking through a crafts market "just looking"? If the answer to these questions is, "Who doesn't?" you fit here. On your vacations, the structure and pace of the day is less important than the particular activities planned.

Look for destinations with a lot of sightseeing and a strong sense of history or local heritage (which may include crafts and cuisine).

Consider: Big cities, foreign destinations, destinations connected with festivals and events.

Relaxation Gurus

Hey, you work hard all week, and so do your kids. If you don't care when anyone wakes up, if your idea of heaven is a margarita, a chaise lounge and a good book, you're a guru. Sure, you'll be willing to open your left eye to make sure that your daughter isn't throwing sand at her cousin, or stir in some time for an activity, but otherwise, you're perfectly content to sit around and chew the fat. Look for destinations that are self-contained and don't require a lot of extra planning once you arrive.

Consider: Beach vacations, countryside getaways, resorts with spas, cruises.

Sports and Adventure Enthusiasts

Is your brain not active if your body isn't moving? Do you use your vacation time to catch up on sporting activities that you don't have time for the rest of the year? No problem. There are plenty of ways to get you pumped, because more than ever, destinations cater to people who take an active approach to life. Beach resorts usually have an abundance of watersports, and many golf resorts also have top-notch tennis facilities. Increasingly, tour operators have picked up on the world's increased awareness of the benefits of exercise.

Instead of driving the French countryside inn-to-inn, you can do an inn-to-inn hike. Bicycle tours are more popular than ever. You can go whitewater rafting. Even hotels have realized that a healthy body means happy guests; gone are the days that a fitness facility was a treadmill and a stationary bike in a dark room—many have built state-of-the-art gyms.

Consider: Beach vacations, ski resorts, golf resorts, national parks, organized adventure tours.

No-Hands Fans

If you think that making decisions all along the trip is going to be miserable, then you may want a vacation that's hands-off—a place where a little planning and decision making (beforehand) goes a long way, and you don't have to think too much once you're there. Opt for places where people can make the most of their own decisions without breaking up the family vacation.

Consider: Cruises, all-inclusives, tours.

CHOOSING A DESTINATION

Once you've identified vacations for your family, it's easy to find out about specific destinations.

Resources

Never before has travel information been so easy to obtain. Try to keep everything you gather organized and in one place in a way that is easily accessible.

On the Web

The Internet has turned everyone into a travel expert. Not only can you retrieve information that was formerly available only in book and magazine form, but you have instant access to periodicals from destinations around the world—all without ever leaving your own home. In addition, every tourist board to almost every destination you can name has a site that will provide not only their own information but links to other helpful sites. Look into tourist board sites; travel operator sites, such as Expedia, Travelocity, CheapTickets, and Orbitz, which not only sell travel, but provide information; and information providers' sites, electronic versions of guidebooks, magazines, newspapers, as well as Web-only sites. Sampling a few sites in all categories will help you get a well-rounded view of every destination you're considering.

Guidebooks

Guidebooks are not supposed to be used only once you've arrived at the destination, but can be a very helpful planning tool before you go. They cover destinations' highlights, but are also full of contact information that has been pre-screened and gathered together to give you a clear and concise picture.

Travel Agents

If you've used a travel agent before, then you have an advantage of having someone at least know your immediate family's travel habits. Agents have tremendous resources at their fingertips and have the advantage of getting feedback from other people who have visited the destination you may have in mind. They can help you come up with destinations as well, but they are most helpful if you come to them as prepared as possible with what you are interested in. The more you know about what your family wants, the more they can do for you. The best agents have specialties; if you don't have an agent you trust (and possibly even if you do), it's worth finding someone who really knows about the type of vacation you're planning. The American Society of Travel Agents is one source of leads; *Conde Nast Traveler* magazine also publishes a list of top agents with varied expertise.

Tour Operators' Brochures

Just looking through the glossy brochures that tour operators send can help you get a clearer idea of where you might want to go. Specifically, if you are going to travel to more than one destination, chances are that a tour operator has already tested tried-and-true routes between them. There's no need to start from scratch, and of course, you can always tailor the itinerary to your own ideas.

Magazines, Newspapers, Television

The minute the seed of the trip is planted, start clipping things that interest you in magazines and newspapers. You can always throw the file out once you've picked your destination, or better yet, save it for the next trip. Once you have chosen a place, keep looking. You'd be amazed how many ideas you can get from articles even if they aren't about your specific spot.

Friends and Family

Word of mouth is a great help, when you're coming down to your final decision. Has anyone you know been there before? Have other family members already gathered information for another trip they were planning? People love to discuss their vacations past and future, so take advantage of what they think.

Narrowing Down Your Choices

Once you've selected various destinations that meet your criteria, it's time to choose the one. All islands are not the same. All resorts are not equally family friendly. Ask some questions of the destination that will help you make sure that it's going to serve your family in the best possible way.

HOW TO PICK A DESTINATION

When evaluating different destinations for your family vacation, consider:

- ☐ Does the destination attract other families?
- ☐ Are there activities for everyone?
- ☐ Are there things to do if it rains?
- ☐ Is there a place for a family party?
- ☐ Do you want to be around other travelers or have privacy?
- ☐ Is the weather consistently good when you'll be there?
- ☐ Are there family activities and dining spots?
- ☐ Are there good medical facilities nearby just in case?
- ☐ Do you know anyone who's been there?

VACATION IDEAS

The following are some tried-and-true destinations that draw families by the millions every year.

City Vacations

Cities are a great option for families of go-goers and culture vultures of different ages and interests. Where else can you find so many different activities in one concentrated area? There's something for almost everyone in your extended family. Big time sports fans can take in a game and shop for team memorabilia. Art lovers can glory in the art, and take in a blockbuster exhibition. Shopaholics can go hog wild. Food lovers can feast on everything from the most refined cuisine by the world's foremost celebrity chefs to simple places where local specialties rule. (Arthur Bryant's barbecue is reason enough to take the whole group to Kansas City.) City playgrounds are often wonderlands for toddlers, while innovative children's museums delight gradeschoolers. The abundance of hotels in all price ranges and the broad range of flights into major metropolitan airports mean that you can find something your clan can afford, no matter what your budget. Even the biggest city in your own region can entertain you, if you haven't been there for a while. Or you could head to one of the coasts—pricewise airfares abound. But don't stop there. Depending on how much time you have, you could consider a city on another continent. Rock-bottom fares in the off season make Europe a possibility. Even your sullen teenager may crack a smile.

Combine activities that involve the whole family and give you shared experiences to talk about, with free time for people to break into groups to pursue their own interests. Stick together for sightseeing and museum tours, sporting events, and concerts and plays. Then go off on your own, only to regroup for a family meal where you can share the events of the day.

12 SPLENDID CITIES YOU'LL LOVE

- [ ] Athens: Soak up the history, then make the resort scene on an island.
- [ ] Chicago: Art, architecture, and the Cubs and White Sox.
- [ ] Las Vegas: Urban buzz for clans without culture vultures; competitive airfares and packages.
- [ ] London: Parks, royalty, theater, great art, history—and they speak English.
- [ ] Los Angeles: Star sightings, theme parks, beaches—the perfect city for outdoors lovers. And it never rains.
- [ ] Montreal: Gambling, jazz, churches, a great exchange rate—and they speak French.
- [ ] New Orleans: For a go-go family that loves jazz, history, and nightlife.
- [ ] New York City: Nirvana not only for culture vultures but also for families, with amazing toddler playgrounds.
- [ ] Rome: Antiquities older than your grandparents, shopping Italian style, and the Vatican. Toss a coin in the fountain and wish to return.
- [ ] San Diego: The big zoo, Legoland, and Shamu.
- [ ] San Francisco: Relive the 60s with your kids and parents amid bay, bridge, hills.
- [ ] Washington, D.C.: A study in civics, diversity, and the greatness of our country.

Beach Vacations

A beach vacation can work for go-goers, relaxation gurus, and sports and adventure enthusiasts alike, providing the perfect balance between an active vacation and a relaxing one. Some of you can swim, snorkel, take windsurfing lessons, go boogie boarding, or play beach volleyball, while others lounge and catch some rays. One or two of you can hit the beach early for some surf-casting—or stay out angling for stripers until dawn. Others can party hearty all night and sleep in until noon. Sand castles, clambakes, family picnics, deep-sea fishing trips, and stargazing can be joint activities.

Sand and water aside, a beach is not just a beach. Some beaches have built-up boardwalks, full of kitschy diversions, while others are sophisticated, good for culture vultures and even shopaholics, and still others are unspoiled stretches of sand. If you have little children,

A BOUQUET OF BEACHES—PICK ONE

On the Atlantic

- [ ] Cape Cod, Massachusetts: Beaches with and without surf, plus ponds, clapboards, wildlife, and much to do when it rains.

- [ ] Nantucket and Martha's Vineyard, Massachusetts: Beachy island idylls.

- [ ] Cape Hatteras, North Carolina: Surf, remote beaches, wildlife, great fishing; same surf as the Cape but overall less expensive.

- [ ] Hilton Head, South Carolina: Wide long beaches, country-club amenities, many well-developed resorts and condo complexes.

- [ ] Palm Beach, Florida: Mansions, old money, ultra-exclusive shopping, Atlantic surf.

On the Gulf

- [ ] Naples, Florida: Fast-growing city with soft white beaches, much shopping and fine arts; Everglades wildlife nearby.

- [ ] Mississippi Gulf Coast: Booming casinos at Biloxi and Gulfport; excursions to National Park beaches from nearby Ocean Springs.

- [ ] South Padre Island, Texas: Seabirds, nature, wide beaches, gentle Gulf waters.

look for your place in the sun along the Gulf Coast, because the water is warm and the surf mild. With middleschoolers or teenagers, go for Atlantic or Pacific

On the Pacific

- [ ] Monterey area, California: Boutiques, galleries, cafés, Pacific surfers, famous golf.
- [ ] Huntington Beach, California: Legendary Pacific surfing and a lively pier.
- [ ] Newport Beach, California: Beaches plus a busy yachting scene, very upscale.
- [ ] Maui, Hawaii: Day trips to Haleakala crater, great golf, planned communities at Kapalua, Kaanapali, Wailea.
- [ ] Kohala Coast, Big Island, Hawaii: Resorts, swimmable beaches, good snorkeling, day hikes in Hawaii Volcanoes National Park.

Caribbean Scenes

- [ ] Aruba: Trade winds whipping down long beaches, plus casinos and high-rise hotels.
- [ ] Barbados: Sugarcane fields, Atlantic *and* Caribbean strands, lingering British flavor.
- [ ] Costa Rica: Many soft, undeveloped beaches, plus fabulous wildlife viewing in a distinctive Latin culture.
- [ ] Jamaica: Lilting island flavor, many all-inclusives, good access from the U.S.
- [ ] St. Barths: Civilized French enclave with crescent beaches, stylish cuisine.

surf. Each beach town has its own flavor and appeal, and finding one that fits your family will ensure a great get-together, whether it be for a long weekend or a two- or three-week vacation.

Wherever you go, make sure you scope out nearby indoor activities, such as museums, historic attractions, a bowling center, or shopping outlets, in case of rain.

A Touring Trip

If your crew is a go-go group, the world *is* your oyster. Pick a place you've always wanted to tour, and go for it. Or look for a point that's convenient to everybody, and see what's nearby. Or pick a theme—Civil War sites, the area where your ancestors lived—and do what it takes to get there. At the same time, consider whether you want to make it a point-to-point trip, where you change hotels every few days or so, or a trip where you make day trips from two successive home bases (probably hotels, motels, inns, or B&Bs) or just one (which could just as well be a rental home).

Depending on your numbers and your destination, you can either contact a tour company to package the trip for you (ideal if you're no-hands fans) or drive your own cars or rent a van or two (if you're not).

One scenario might play out like this: You're no-hands fans and you're not constrained by budget, so you put together a safari tour. Or hire a tour company to plan a coach tour through Russia to St. Petersburg (because you've always wanted to see this grand city) and to a couple of villages a few hours away, where your great-great-grandparents were born and died.

Or, if there aren't enough of you to make a group, you all sign up with another group that has space.

Or, let's say your ancestors migrated west along the Oregon Trail. You fly into St. Louis, rent a 15-passenger van for the eight of you, and go westward from place to place visiting historic sites that showcase how the pioneers lived, and venturing down byways where you can still see ruts left over from the days wagon trains took settlers into the wild, wild west.

Here's another example. You're go-goers and culture vultures and your mom has always dreamed of touring Tuscany. You want to take her and your dad to Italy before they are too old to travel. But you have small kids. So you rent a couple of cars and a villa with a swimming pool in the hills above Volterra and make day trips to churches and hill towns nearby. You shop in the local market and cook meals yourself while your kids are splashing in the pool and your parents are sipping a glass of wine, watching them and soaking up the view.

Touring Tips

As they say, if you can dream it, you can do it. A touring trip will put you out there together sharing experiences and building your relationship at the same time. That's the good news. The bad news is that a touring trip enforces a certain degree of togetherness, and as travelers often learn, traveling with people you know well is tough—life on the road has a way of illuminating new faces of even old friends. So before you invest a lot of money in a big trip together, schedule a long weekend jaunt to some destination that's convenient to all of you, so that you can see whether you will be as compatible as traveling companions as you are as family.

With kids, touring with mom and dad at the helm is often harder than going as part of a guided tour—kids who dispute everything their parents tell them to do will often fall into line when their marching orders come from the tour guide.

If you do sign up for a group tour, make sure you know exactly what's included and beware of hidden costs. Are taxes, tips, and service charges included? Transfers and baggage handling? Entertainment and excursions? These can add up. Also find out what's extra.

Prices for packages and tours are usually quoted per person, based on two sharing a room. Most of the time, one of the biggest differences among tours pricewise is in accommodations, which run from budget to better and better to best. People in your group who are traveling solo may be required to pay the full double-occupancy rate. Some operators eliminate this surcharge if the singles agree to be matched with a roommate of the same sex, even if one is not found by departure time.

TRAVEL LOG

My extended family has rented vacation homes a few times in small wine villages in Bordeaux in southwest France. We rent a car, but mostly take family bike trips during the day along country roads through vineyards to neighboring villages. Each little village has street markets on different days in summer, which are perfect for shopping and people-watching. We enjoy the wines of the area, as well as nearby Cognac's famous brandy and Roquefort's well-known cheese. Occasionally we drive out to the beaches on the Atlantic Coast, or to some of France's most famous sites, such as Roman excavations and aqueducts in nearby Toulouse and Carcassonne.

—*Kate R., New York, New York*

Cruises

Several family-friendly features may make a cruise ideal for a multigenerational trip. Stateroom accommodations are often better suited than hotel rooms to an extended family because so many sleeping configurations, price categories, and optional amenities exist. Different family segments can choose cabin accommodations based on their needs and budget. Dining rooms often have a wide range of choices, children's menus, vegetarian dishes, and, in most cases, staff able to cater to special dietary needs. The high ratio of cruise-ship staff to passengers means that service is normally attentive for everyone in your family. You'll usually find staff members on board who specialize in children's activities, while other ship employees arrange activities for older guests. Finally, the huge array of options means that you can find a cruise to suit everyone in the group—and negotiate some very good deals.

At various ports of call your family can usually opt for one of several different choices. You can all leave the ship on an organized tour, venture out on your own, or arrange ahead for your own driver-guide. Or you can break up into groups and pursue your own interests, and then meet up again back on the ship.

You can cruise in Alaska, in the Caribbean, or the Mediterranean; take a ferry up the coast of Norway; or board a paddlewheeler to steam up or down the mighty Mississippi on the trail of Huck Finn.

A Cruise to Fit Your Family

Keep in mind that cruise ships vary by size, style, and accommodations. Large luxury liners carry more than 1,000 passengers and are often packed with diversions like discos and casinos. Smaller expedition vessels may carry only 100 passengers and may have lectures and libraries instead of nightlife. Is a full program of organized activities scheduled by day? What happens in the evening? What kind of entertainment is offered after dark? And how often do passengers dress up for dinner? Some cruises are fancier than others. Make a list of your family's priorities, talk to friends who've taken cruises, and otherwise do your homework.

Evaluate Onboard Amenities

Discuss the services and facilities your family requires, and evaluate each ship carefully. Don't assume that all facilities are the same. Consider pools. Most ships have at least one, but the quality and size of the pool can make or break a sunshine cruise. Avoid large ships with small pools, where on a hot day the pool can seem like an overcrowded bathtub. Make sure there are pools and enough hot tubs on deck to accommodate adult passengers and a good kids' pool for your small fry.

Dining

Before selecting a cruise, discuss dining arrangements with your family. Traditional cruises usually have one somewhat formal main dining area, where you'll be assigned a set dining time and set tables for the duration of the cruise. If your extended family wants to dine together in one large group every evening, this is a good option.

Find out whether there are one or two seatings in the dining room. If there is more than one, you will not be allowed to arrive and exit as the spirit moves you but instead will be expected to show up promptly when service begins and clear out within a specified time. The first seating will probably be preferable if you have a number of young children in your group—and in fact many ships with two dinner seatings routinely assign passengers with children to the earlier seating. Some lines will not permit children to eat in the dining room on their own. If your kids are picky eaters, check ahead to see if special children's menus are offered; many lines offer them. If you need a high chair, request it in advance.

If your family might want to break up into different groups and eat when the spirit moves you, opt for a newer ship with several alternative restaurants. Note that some of these ships charge a small service fee for these restaurants-at-sea.

Start with a Good Agent

Perhaps the best way to shop for a cruise is to decide first on a cruise ship that has the right features for your family, and then to shop for an agency. Most agencies have partnerships with certain cruise lines, which can work to your advantage. By agreeing to sell a lot of cabins (and, of course, promoting certain cruise lines), the agency gets a better rate from them. The agency can then afford to offer a "discounted" price to the public. Know the affiliations of any agency you choose.

Equally important when you book your family's cruise, use a travel agent who's an expert in the field.

The best agencies can get you cabin upgrades and provide 24-hour service in case of a problem. The most qualified agents are members of the Cruise Lines International Association (CLIA); those who are CLIA Accredited Cruise Counsellors and Master Cruise Counsellors have had extensive cruise and ship-inspection experience. If you opt for a cruise-specialist agency, make sure it is a member of the National Association of Cruise Oriented Agencies. A good cruise agent will ask you many detailed questions about your past vacations, your lifestyle, and even your friends and your hobbies. Never book a cruise with an agent who asks only a few cursory questions before handing you a brochure.

More Cruise Tips

If there are first-time cruisers and families with children in your group, look for a short cruise—a three- or four-day sailing to the Bahamas or Key West and Cozumel out of Miami or, from Los Angeles, a three- or four-day cruise down the southern California coast to Baja, in Mexico. Short itineraries may include stops at one or two ports of call, or none at all.

If some members of your family have limited mobility, look for a ship whose public rooms are clustered on one deck. Several cruise lines have reduced rates for senior citizens (sometimes only on certain sailings), and seniors may be able to take advantage of local discounts ashore.

With Kids

If you have children in your group, look for a ship and line that's family friendly. While there may be free passage for children on special off-peak sailings, typically most cruise lines charge children under age 12 third- and fourth-passenger rates or children's fares when they are traveling with two adults in the same cabin. These rates tend to be about half—sometimes even less than half—of the lowest adult fare.

Be sure to find out how the kids' program is set up. The best separate children into different age groups. On the two Disney cruise ships, *Disney Magic* and *Disney Wonder,* for instance, dozens of counselors handle children in four different age groups. Younger groups have a clubhouse, a pirate ship, arts and crafts, and much more; older children can access science areas and computers and undertake detailed art projects. Teens can make a movie, play sports, or hang out in a New York-style coffeehouse.

Look into how many hours of supervised activities are scheduled each day, whether meals are included, and what the counselor-to-child ratio is (a 1 to 3 ratio is ideal when younger children are involved). Some ships provide day care and group baby-sitting for younger children at no extra charge, while most charge a nominal hourly rate. On many ships, private baby-sitting is by arrangement with crew members (at a negotiated price).

Other cruises provide similar facilities for children, but some provide only child care—but no organized activities.

If there are infants and toddlers in your crew, be sure to ask about age requirements. Some cruise ships don't allow infants aboard, period; others require a minimum age, anywhere from 4 to 18 months. Find out exactly what the cruise line provides (some supply diapers, formula, and baby food free of charge) and plan accordingly.

Alumni Clubs

After your cruise, join the line's alumni club if you think your extended family might want to take a cruise together again in the future. You'll receive newsletters with notice of discounts on future cruises, some as much as 50% below brochure prices. Everyone must sign up for the alumni club to take advantage of the discounts.

Theme Parks

If a few of you gave high marks on your survey to variety shows and thrill rides, there may be a theme park in your future. Although roller coaster lovers need no more encouragement than the thought of a twisting mass of steel track to pack up and go, theme parks lend themselves to family gatherings for one other big reason: there's a lot to share. Most parks have been planned specifically to appeal to a broad range of interests, so apart from the wild rides there are gentle ones that please young children, older travelers, and more sedate types. Some parks include animal displays. Most regale you with lively musical entertainment with lots of audience participation. It's a rare child who isn't totally delighted by what theme parks offer—and that alone provides enjoyment to the people in the group who manage to remain unmoved by the rest of the package. Plus, many attractions in many theme parks are completely accessible to people who use wheelchairs or have other disabilities.

Finally theme parks are everywhere, from coast to coast (although with concentrations in Orlando and southern California), and the areas around them are full of hotels and motels in all shapes, styles, and price categories. Because both the theme parks and the nearby associated lodgings tend to do a lot of group business, no one will say, "Huh?" if you want a group deal on a crowd of 55. Although theme park admissions alone can be pricey, multi-day packages are always available, and these include the admission along with accommodations and possibly transportation and some meals. Some packages to some parks include such bonuses as early entry to the park.

Since long lines, heat, humidity, and sensory overload are more or less constant—and can wear down some older travelers—you can divide your crew into posses and split up to pursue your separate interests. (Hint: Start out every day with a couple of different rendezvous points and times, just in case you get separated accidentally.) In any case, some of you may decide to spend the afternoon around your hotel swimming pool, anyway.

Around Orlando

If your family is looking for maximum theme park excitement in one destination, look no farther than Orlando, Florida, the epicenter of the theme park world. When most people think of this central Florida city, they think of Walt Disney World, but the area is also home to several other fun-packed parks, and Disney itself is much more than just cartoon characters and rides. WDW also includes not only four theme parks (the Magic Kingdom, with the Cinderella Castle in the middle, plus an animal park, a movie park, and the educational theme park, Epcot) but also several resorts. After dark, a huge array of family nightlife options cranks up. The Downtown Disney and Pleasure Island complexes are packed with restaurants, concert venues, shops, and nightclubs. Downtown Disney is also home to a permanent show by the innovative, no-animals circus known as Cirque du Soleil.

Nearby Universal Orlando packs in thrill rides and entertainment in two parks. Universal Studios Florida gives you intense rides and stunt shows based on films such as *Jaws, Back to the Future,* and *Twister.* Islands of Adventure theme park is an even more dizzying collection of roller coasters, water rides, and special effects, with such characters as Spider-Man, the Jurassic Park dinosaurs, and the Incredible Hulk. The CityWalk nightlife-and-dining complex between the two parks is Universal's answer to Downtown Disney. And there are some pretty nifty places to stay, including a Hard Rock Hotel.

Beyond Universal and Disney is SeaWorld Orlando, a marine theme park where you and the gang can get splashed by a killer whale, touch sting rays, ride some wild rides, and catch some lively shows. SeaWorld's Discovery Cove park, next door, is like a water park with animal interactions—you can snorkel with sting rays and swim with the dolphins (and you'll pay dearly for this priceless experience). Busch Gardens Tampa, with still more coasters and a bounty of animal exhibits, is just an hour's drive away on Florida's West Coast. Cape Canaveral is the same distance in the opposite direction. And all of this is going strong all year round.

Southern California

Southern California is another stellar option for theme park lovers. There are two Disney parks, the original Disneyland—smaller, more intimate than its Florida cousin—and the new California Adventure. Not far away, you'll find a whole host of other parks, including Six Flags Magic Mountain in Valencia, Six

Flags Marine World in Vallejo, Knott's Berry Farm, Legoland, and other venues, each different and distinctive. But there are other real-life attractions in the area as well, including beaches, Hollywood, and the Getty Center. The competitive lodging scene should yield good bargain hunting. So if you're a go-go family with a culture-vulture streak but you like a good day on the beach as well as the next guy, this area warrants your consideration.

Regional Theme Parks

If neither Orlando nor southern California are nearby and no one in your family is up for a long trip, consider one of the nation's many regional amusement parks. In general these are open only when the weather is warm, and they're not self-contained resort destinations like Walt Disney World and Universal. Instead, they make for vacations on the southern California model, providing city vacations with some coaster thrills thrown in. Many have adjacent water parks.

Because these parks draw from all over their regions, you'll find an abundance of lodging—mostly modern and short on character (at least compared to the highly themed hostelries in Walt Disney World), but perfectly serviceable. After all, when all is said and done, it may be the hotel pool and their newfound cousins that kids remember with most affection.

A THEME PARK WHEREVER YOU ARE

- ☐ Colorado: Six Flags Elitch Gardens, an old-timer, near Denver.
- ☐ Georgia: Six Flags Over Georgia, near Atlanta.
- ☐ Illinois: Six Flags Great America, near Chicago at Gurnee.
- ☐ Kentucky: Six Flags Kentucky Kingdom, near Louisville.
- ☐ Louisiana: Jazzland, themed around nearby New Orleans.
- ☐ Maryland: Six Flags America, near Largo.
- ☐ Massachusetts: Six Flags New England, near Springfield.
- ☐ Missouri: Six Flags St. Louis.
- ☐ New Jersey: Six Flags Great Adventure, near Jackson.
- ☐ Ohio: Cedar Point, Sandusky, America's roller-coaster capital. King's Island, near Cincinnati, with costumed characters like Yogi Bear and the Flintstones. Six Flags Worlds of Adventure, near Aurora, with marine attractions and rides.
- ☐ Pennsylvania: Dorney Park & Wildwater Kingdom, Allentown. Hershey Park, Hershey, thrill rides with chocolate in the air.
- ☐ Texas: Six Flags Astroworld, near Houston, and Six Flags Over Texas at Arlington, near Dallas.
- ☐ Virginia: Paramount's Kings Dominion, near Richmond, home of the East Coast's largest roller coaster.

Winter Sports Vacations

A winter sports vacation can be a wonderful experience for young and old. That's first of all because skiing and snowboarding are such great equalizers. With instruction, gradeschoolers and middleschoolers can keep up with their parents; if they keep it up, by the time they hit their rebellious years, they are usually way ahead of their mothers and often their fathers as well. Fueled by the shared experiences and made closer by enforced quiet time together on the chairlift, relationships flourish. If yours is a household that loves winter sports, it might be fun to introduce the idea to your extended family as well.

On a winter sports trip, you will bond on the basis of shared abilities or shared experiences. Experts will share the bumps together, while beginners share their bunny-slope tumbles and intermediates celebrate—together—having challenged and conquered the occasional black diamond. Although you may all start the day together, once you're on the slopes, groups will form, break up, and reform by the hour. You rendezvous for a lunch (on the early side, the better to snag a table together) and for drinks afterwards, then all regroup again at your hotel.

Almost every winter sports resort has a huge variety of places to stay, including houses and condos for rent by the month or by the week as well as hotels and resorts. You'll also find B&Bs, ranches, or other one-of-a-kind properties, and ski lodges—casual places designed to foster togetherness. In winter sports country, many hostelries have a complement of public spaces that invite hanging out. Good ones have nooks for kids, teens, and adults alike.

Fun for Never-Befores and Never-Evers

And what of the more sedentary members of your crew? Depending on the area, there may be shopping, spas, indoor tennis courts, wildlife watching, even sights to see. Family members who don't ski or snowboard may rediscover the pleasures of reading a good book in front of a fire in a quiet lodge. In dry years, when there's no snow on the trails, there's hiking; there's cross-country skiing in other years (and at resorts that have snowmaking at their cross-country skiing areas). And who knows—the never-befores in your crew may decide to challenge the bunny slope.

Issues to Consider

First find out how many actually want to join you on the slopes (and what their ability levels are). Equipped with that knowledge, you're ready to look for a resort that matches your group profile—in the Rockies or the Alps, New England or California or beyond. If there are beginners in your group, you may also want to consider Michigan or West Virginia. And pay special attention to the ski school; best of all is the kind where you stay with a single group when you sign up

WINTER RESORTS TO CONSIDER

Some Snowy Spots in the East

- [ ] Mad River Valley, Vermont: Behemoth Sugarbush for boarders, plus tiny Mad River when the snow's good.
- [ ] Okemo, Vermont: Ballroom territory for intermediates, the East's best snowmaking.
- [ ] Snowshoe, West Virginia: Small but mighty fun for families.

A Bit of the Wild, Wild West

- [ ] Snowmass, Colorado: One of the giants of the West, loaded with ski-in/ski-out lodging and a pedestrian village at the base, a stone's throw from ultracosmopolitan Aspen.
- [ ] Taos, New Mexico: A small resort with a big mountain with steep slopes, intimate lodges, and southwestern culture nearby.
- [ ] Vail, Colorado: Vast terrain and a faux-Alpine village a hop down I-70 from Denver.
- [ ] Whistler, British Columbia: Big mountains and big resorts, with many options—and an affordable exchange rate.

A Few Alpine Options

- [ ] Kitzbühel, Austria: One of the great alpine destinations, with stylish hotels and something for everyone on and off the mountain.
- [ ] Obergurgl, Austria: A quiet, isolated alpine village with snow well into spring.
- [ ] Zermatt, Switzerland: In the shadow of the Matterhorn, with beginner terrain way up top, with all the views.

for a week of lessons. Depending on your gang's ability levels and numbers, some ski schools will let you form your own class.

If there are young children, make sure the resort area has child-care facilities to take care of kids the age of yours; some accept kids only after they're potty-trained, while others offer nonskiing programs for the wee ones and a play program with some skiing for three-year-olds and above. Bigger places have more options.

You may want to look for smaller places where all trails funnel back to one spot, particularly if there are no serious hotshots among you. Although this kind of area won't offer the huge variety of slopes and trails of a bigger one, there are benefits. When the area isn't too large, older gradeschoolers can go off in groups on their own, in a brief bit of independence that they love, and it's easy for everyone to meet up at the end of a run. A small ski area in a region of big mountains can give you the best of both worlds.

Consistent snow is an issue. Because you will probably be booking your vacation far in advance, you may or may not luck out with the snow. Many resorts in New England make snow for 100% of their trails, so as long as the weather is cold enough, snow is guaranteed. Elsewhere it varies. In Europe, for instance, there may be snow up high, but not down below; you'll ski, but you won't find those endless runs from above treeline through pastures and forests and into the village that make the European ski experience so distinctive.

It's worth noting that for the last few years, European ski destinations have been offering very competitive packages that include airfare, accommodations, lift tickets, and free local transportation, so that when you ski from one village to another, as is frequently done in Europe, you get free bus or train transportation back to your home base. That said, it's also true that most major American ski resorts also offer a huge variety of packages and all welcome the group business. Do price out a few options (including air travel to and from the destination as well as ground arrangements), and don't dismiss bigger and farther-away places until you have considered all costs to determine that they really are out of your price range.

Camping and Hiking

An extended-family gathering around a campfire—complete with s'mores and silly songs—can be a wonderful bonding experience. Every state has a network of state parks, many with campsites for trailers and tents. Private campgrounds are another option. Kampgrounds of America (KOA) maintains high standards at its campgrounds nationwide. Clean facilities, a well-stocked camp store, a good swimming pool, and a playground are the norm.

CAN YOU STOP GIGGLING?

One of the pleasures of camping with your extended family is gathering around the campfire in a noisy, festive crowd. However, because all campers are sharing close quarters, many campgrounds observe quiet time. When you're exploring campgrounds, ask when quiet time begins—it may be 9, 10, or 11—and make sure you're comfortable with the rule. Although it may not mean lights out, you will probably have to turn off your music, lower your voices, and quiet your dogs—and your laughter.

Most parks have hiking trails, swimming and boating areas, and other recreational facilities. Local outfitters can take your family on kayaking, rafting, hiking, and horseback riding excursions. After dark, you can plan games, charades, and sing-alongs. And don't forget to pack marshmallows, graham crackers, and chocolate bars.

Cross-Country

If your family has a month or more of travel time to spare and you can't zero in on one destination, why not drive across the country in a recreational vehicle? You'll have a chance to visit some of the country's best sights, from the Grand Canyon to the Adirondacks. Depending on the season, you might cross the country

10 GREAT OPTIONS OUTDOORS

National Parks

- [ ] Grand Canyon, Arizona: The one-and-only.

- [ ] Rocky Mountain National Park, Colorado: The quintessential Rockies, with outdoor experiences within the abilities of everyone.

- [ ] Yellowstone, sprawling across Montana and Wyoming: Immense and wonderful year around; a steamy, hot-and-cold wonderland under snow.

- [ ] Yosemite, California: Go in summer or reserve way, way, ahead for the Bracebridge Dinner, the famous Yuletide costumed feast, then go cross-country skiing together.

- [ ] Zion and Bryce Canyon, Utah: Stunning red-rock desert.

National Forests

- [ ] Black Hills, South Dakota: The rugged gulches and rough hills, rising over the prairies, exerted a spiritual pull on native Americans that you can feel today.

- [ ] Kaibab, Arizona: Flanking the Grand Canyon, with deserts, pine forests, and alpine terrain.

- [ ] Sierra, California: Giant sequoias without the crowds, angling in the Merced River, hiking in the John Muir wilderness.

- [ ] Superior, Minnesota: For the lush and splendid forests, superb fishing.

- [ ] White Mountain, New Hampshire: A hut-to-hut hike along the Appalachian Trail in the Presidential Range area makes for a never-to-be-forgotten bonding experience.

in one direction on a northern route and return home taking a southern route to visit the most sights.

If you don't own a recreational vehicle, rent one. Vehicles range widely in size and amenities, with everything from retractable beds that turn into tables to entertainment units and microwave ovens. Campgrounds charge about $25 to $35 per night, depending on location, for an overnight site with electric and water hookups. Consider towing a compact car behind your RV so you can run errands and take small trips without having to take your temporary home with you.

TRAVEL LOG

When we drove a motor home cross-country, we hitched up a small car for convenience. It turned out to be a big help when our motor home broke down. Instead of having to wait for help to show up, two of us drove into town to seek assistance and supplies while the others stayed with the vehicle. While waiting for the mobile home to be repaired, we were able to take off in the car and do some sightseeing, which eased some of the disappointment of the breakdown. Having the extra car saved us a lot of time and trouble.

—*Edward L., Las Vegas, Nevada*

---

106 PLACES TO GO, THINGS TO DO

ALTERNATIVE VACATIONS

Maybe you're looking for something a little different for this family vacation—perhaps a wide-open space with fewer crowds, or a part of the country that's new to your family.

City Slickers on Open Prairies

Ever since Billy Crystal donned a pair of chaps in the film *City Slickers,* dude ranch visits have been popular family attractions in parts of Colorado, Arizona, New Mexico, Wyoming, Montana, and Utah. Horseback riding, chuck wagon camp-outs, mock cattle drives, mini-rodeos, and all meals and lodgings complete the Wild West fantasy. You can check in for a week, or buy a package that also includes river rafting, ghost town tours, or guided backpacking trips.

Because ranches vary, it's important to do your homework before choosing one, and to take into consideration the age and energy level of all your family members. Some ranches have children's programs; others are adults-only during certain periods. Some ranches are geared to riders, while others have many additional activities.

Bonding on the Fairway

The golf bug runs in many families. If your family consists of serious players and beginners, let the serious golfers book an early tee time and rejoin the family by early afternoon. If you plan on playing together, try to book the last tee time so other people won't have to wait behind your family.

Consider a golf resort with spa facilities, especially if some of your relatives have no interest in the sport. While part of your family group plays golf, the rest can relax at the spa or by the pool. Or you can all golf one day and indulge yourselves at the spa the next. And note that while single-day golf outings can be pricey, you can save considerably by purchasing a multiday package with accommodations.

Golf Schools

Many top golf resorts focus on adult beginners with nongolf activities for children, but at some resorts you can arrange for family golf lessons. U.S. Schools of Golf and U.S. Sports Camps have nationwide parent-child golf camps where it is also possible to arrange private group lessons for family groups. You usually start the day on the driving range then move onto the course to challenge a few holes in the company of an instructor. Programs last two or three days, and packages can include hotel accommodations. Rates range

THE FRONT NINE: TOP GOLF GETAWAYS

- [ ] Kona-Kohala Coast, Hawaii: Superb Pacific's-edge golf resorts with ocean and mountain views.

- [ ] Maui, Hawaii: With scenery like this, how do you keep your mind on the game? Several layouts here are legendary; municipal courses expand your options at moderate cost.

- [ ] Myrtle Beach, South Carolina: The self-styled golf capital of the world, with nearly 100 courses, many lodging options and serious beach.

- [ ] Orlando, Florida: Golfers can putt guilt-free knowing that the rest of the clan is with Mickey or Shamu.

- [ ] Palm Springs, California: More than 95 courses, many of which you've seen on TV. Golf widows can soak up the incessant sunshine by the pool.

- [ ] Monterey, California: Spyglass Hill and Pebble Beach Golf Links are iconic, pine-and-ocean challenges.

- [ ] Naples, Florida: Many courses and Gulf surf.

- [ ] Pinehurst, North Carolina: Home of the World Golf Hall of Fame.

- [ ] San Diego, California: A golf-mad city, with near-perfect weather year-round.

- [ ] Scottsdale, Arizona: As good as golf can be on more than 174 courses, with near-daily sunshine; home of the great Nicklaus/Flick golf school.

Alternative Vacations

from $200 to $250 per person per day (not including accommodations). A light breakfast and lunch are included with lessons.

River Rafting

Professional outfitters from West Virginia to California can guide your family on a rafting trip to suit your interests and abilities. The thrills you'll share will bring everyone closer. Tours range from a few hours to a multinight camping journey on the Colorado River, and often include hiking and fishing. Trips geared to families usually take you through easy to moderate white water (Class I–Class III) appropriate for young children, and they can include storytellers, naturalists, and off-river activities counselors.

Choose a reputable outfitter with a proven track record. The best are certified; check with the certifying group to verify the outfitter's record before signing up. Also talk to a few past guests to scope out the trip's style. Some outfitters pamper you with fine food and even live chamber music under the stars; others have you pitch in with cooking and clean-up.

Volunteering

Even though you pay your own way to do volunteer work and sleep in dormitory-style accommodations, working with your family to help humanity is a gratifying way to spend your vacation. Opportunities range

10 GREAT RIVERS WORTH RAFTING

- [ ] The Colorado through the Grand Canyon, Arizona: The grandest scenery of all, plus 200 rapids.
- [ ] The Colorado through Cataract Canyon, Utah: Roaring whitewater and red-rocks scenery.
- [ ] The Green River and the Yampa, Utah: Through Dinosaur National Monument on mostly Class II–III waters.
- [ ] The Main Salmon, Idaho: Big whitewater and unspoiled wilderness, with wide beaches for camping.
- [ ] The Middle Fork of the Salmon, Idaho: Primitive and untouched, with Class IV–V white-water. One of the eight original Wild and Scenic Rivers.
- [ ] Snake River through Hells Canyon, Idaho: Through the country's deepest chasm, with Class III–IV whitewater and good fishing.
- [ ] The Snake River, Wyoming: Placid Class I waters, perfect for first-timers, with the Tetons towering above.
- [ ] The Rogue, Oregon: Big, full, and fast; especially satisfying for wildlife lovers. Class III–III+.
- [ ] The Tatshenshini, Alaska: Some of the wildest and remotest river country in North America, with amazing scenery.
- [ ] The San Juan, Utah: Petroglyphs and pottery shards, with Class II rapids.

Alternative Vacations

from overseas trips to help various communities to building homes through charitable organizations to maintaining wilderness areas.

Through Habitat for Humanity, for example, your family can join trips to either U.S. or international destinations to help build houses. Each trip lasts two or three weeks.

You pay travel costs plus a base fee of about $350 per participant to cover living expenses at the site. No children under 17 are permitted, but there is no upper age limit. Habitat's most famous active member is former president Jimmy Carter, now in his late seventies.

Other organizations with international volunteer travel opportunities are Global Volunteers, a United Nations-affiliated group with projects in 19 countries, and Volunteers for Peace, with two- to three-week volunteer camps in 70 countries, including a few European camps that accept family-group volunteers. Although Volunteers for Peace accepts volunteers of all ages, including children under 18 in some destinations, the trips are best for adults.

4

Getting the Show on the Road

GETTING THERE MAY NOT BE HALF THE FUN, but it can be enjoyable no matter how large your group. So what's your mode of transport? Are you traveling by plane? Taking a six-hour car ride to the mountains? A cross-country train trip? Wherever you're going and however you get there, successfully traveling with an extended family involves a few extra considerations above and beyond the usual transportation concerns.

Start planning early, and book flights or rental cars at least several months ahead or even a year in advance for large groups and popular destinations. The longer you let your transportation arrangements slide, the harder it will be for you to get what you want for your family.

AIR TRAVEL

If your group is large and scattered across the country, let each household make its own air-travel arrangements. But you or your family negotiator should still search out discount group rates from an airline that serves your family's various home cities. Contact the group sales department of a few different airlines and have them submit bids for your group. If your extended family consists of 20 or more members, seek fares at least one-third below published prices for individual travelers. The larger your group, the larger the discount you can expect.

Once you confirm the group rate, which may include surcharges for those flying longer distances, you'll be given a booking code for your group. Have each household call the airline's reservation number and use the code to book tickets at the agreed group rate.

A travel agent can also help you negotiate a group rate. Most large agencies maintain preferred relationships with certain carriers and can get you a better rate based on the agency's booking volume with the airline. As few as 10 passengers can qualify for a group discount.

Sharing Frequent Flier Awards

Rules are specific and vary by carrier on how family members can share frequent flier miles. In most cases, you can have frequent flier mileage awards issued to a member of your immediate family. However, different family members usually cannot combine miles from their separate accounts to qualify for an award. Contact your airline for all the details.

The individual frequent-flier program member must redeem his or her miles directly with the airline. Award travel is somewhat restricted and subject to blackout rules that don't apply to the group-discount program. So an individual family member using mileage can *try* to book the same flight as the group, but there is no guarantee of getting it. If the flight is not available, the family member has the choice of either paying the group rate or using the miles to get a different flight.

Airport Shuttle

Your family can save itself the hassle of driving and parking multiple cars by using an airport-shuttle service, and you can sometimes negotiate discount rates for your group. Have everyone who lives in the same town converge on one or two houses before departure

REQUIRED TRAVEL DOCUMENTS

Send a list of necessary travel documents to each household a few weeks before you depart. If you're visiting a destination that requires passports and visas, make sure everyone acquires the necessary documents in advance.

- ☐ A government-issued photo I.D., even when it's not required; a passport is best.

- ☐ A valid birth certificate for children younger than driving age; school-age children should also bring a student I.D. card, especially if it has a photo.

- ☐ For a noncustodial parent, a notarized letter from a child's custodial parent providing permission for travel across state or international borders.

- ☐ Any necessary visas.

- ☐ Vaccination papers from your doctor for some international destinations.

time. Schedule pickup service half an hour before you'd normally depart, and reconfirm your departure time the day before you travel.

After a long trip, who wants to pile into four or five different cabs or rental cars to get to your destination? Spending a little extra to arrange for a meet-and-greet service upon your arrival at the vacation destination can save you some stress. So pay for a guided van service to pick you up. The greeter, whom you can hire through your hotel, travel agent, or sometimes through the local tourist office, normally meets you in the baggage claim area with a sign. The cost for your large group may even equal cab fare.

At the Airport

With a large group flying out of the same airport, give yourselves extra time to get there and check in smoothly. Ask your carrier about its check-in policy. You're usually required to arrive at the airport about 90 minutes to two hours before your scheduled departure time for domestic flights and two-and-a-half to three hours before international flights. To accommodate a large group's needs—everything from multiple bathroom breaks to snack purchases—add a half hour. Ensuring that the preflight time is unhurried sets a good tone for the vacation.

The Airport Wait

For most people, time spent at the airport ranks right up there with a visit to the dentist. And if you're gathering in a large family group, the experience can be even worse, especially if you've got lots of children or a complainer in your family.

Break up a group into smaller ones if you have a long wait ahead. This way some family members can head for the shops, others can sit and read in the lounge, and still others can go for snacks. Stick to no more than two or three groups, each with at least one adult, to reduce the risk of members getting lost; if you've got a few cell phones in your family, divide them up among the different groups so you can stay in contact. Set a designated meeting time at your gate, and make sure each family household has a designated ticket holder.

Prepare for delays by packing magazines, snacks, a deck of cards, and a travel game. Stifle the grumblers and start the family fun early. Claim a corner of the terminal lounge to yourselves and play a quiet game or start catching up. Designate one family member to communicate with airline boarding-gate or check-in personnel.

Keeping Kids Moving

Long airport lines can make even the most patient of people fidgety, so imagine how tough it is on young kids with lots of energy and short attention spans. If kids grow cranky and rambunctious, send them off for a stroll with another adult while a few family members hold the place in line and look after the baggage. Let the people behind you in the check-in line know what you are doing so they accept the rest of the family back without a fuss. Kids can visit shops and pick up a small toy for the plane ride. Keep in touch by cell phone, and make sure everyone's back in line in time for your family to check in together.

CHILDREN'S ONBOARD SURVIVAL KITS

- ☐ Snacks.
- ☐ Paper towels or wet wipes for messes and spills, in a resealable plastic bag.
- ☐ Water bottles.
- ☐ Coloring or activity book, crayons, colored pencils.
- ☐ Card game.
- ☐ Small stuffed animal or doll.
- ☐ Flight map.
- ☐ Personal CD players, video games, CDs.
- ☐ Extra batteries.
- ☐ Pacifiers and blankets for babies.

THE RUBBER-TIRE VACATION

Who doesn't have fond memories of the family car trip? The anticipation, the scenery, the car games, the car-travel question sine qua non: "Are we there yet?" OK, maybe your memories are a mixed bag: there's a lot that can be fun on a family car trip, and a lot that can go wrong. The trick is to plan carefully and address potentially stressful situations before they arise.

With your extended family, you'll likely have to take several different cars. This will introduce some new

ESSENTIALS FOR YOUR CAR

- [ ] Cell phone numbers of other family members.
- [ ] Phone number at your next destination.
- [ ] Driving directions for your family's route.
- [ ] Music tapes or CDs; books on tape.
- [ ] Tool kit.
- [ ] Extra water; windshield-wiper fluid.
- [ ] Motor oil; coolant or anti-freeze.
- [ ] Spare tire.
- [ ] Cooler with drinks and snacks.
- [ ] Maps.
- [ ] Your auto-club membership card.

challenges. You'll need to coordinate rendezvous stops and drive at approximately the same speed. Make sure each car in your family caravan has a cell phone so you can stay in touch. Keep the trip interesting by rotating family members among the different vehicles at rest stops.

The Navigator

Appoint a navigator—someone with a good sense of direction and a knack with maps—to be your guide. The navigator should study the route in advance, write down the sequence of roads to follow, and plan alternate routes, especially around major cities, in case you run into accidents or congestion. You also need good maps for every car; you should have good state and city maps with local roads marked in case you need or want to get off the main highway.

The navigator should explain the route to and stay in touch with one member of each car to make sure everyone's on the same page.

Rendezvous Stops

Instead of trying to follow one another closely, plan to rendezvous at designated rest areas at set times. If all cars start out on the trip together and no one drives unusually fast or slow, you should arrive at rest stops at approximately the same time. Keep in touch by cell phone.

Many rest stops have grassy areas with picnic tables. Instead of springing for fast food, pack a cooler ahead of time and enjoy a family picnic. Walk around a bit, and make sure the kids take a bathroom break.

Family Car Games

The following car games help pass the driving time:

The Geography Game. One person names a place—a state, city, country, continent, river, or ocean—and the next person has to come up with a place whose name starts with the last letter of the first place. If Dad starts out with "Georgia," Uncle Al might follow with "Antwerp," and Aunt Mildred with "Paris." Keep taking turns until you run out of places.

Trivia. Pack up some Trivial Pursuit cards and have a trivia contest. Play "Who Wants to Be a Millionaire?" and let family members serve as "lifelines."

Character Stories. The first player spots a person in another car and makes up a story describing who the character is, where he or she is going, and why. Each player takes a turn picking a person in a different car and continuing the story. You earn extra points for linking characters in the same plot.

The Slug Bug Game. Have all car passengers keep their eyes peeled for Volkswagen Beetles on the road. Whenever someone spots a Beetle, he or she should shout out "Slug Bug [color of car]." The person who calls out first wins a point. Score extra points for people who spot the old Beetles from the 1960s and 1970s.

Breaking up the Trip

Kids and adults get antsy, fatigued, and irritable during long drives. One way to keep everyone sane is to break a long trip into two major segments, with an overnight stay in between. Eating an early dinner and getting a good night's rest are the key to the next day's travel success.

RENTAL-CAR EXTRAS TO PRICE OUT

When figuring the cost of a rental vehicle, take into consideration all the extras:

- [ ] Collision- or loss-damage waiver: Always optional, it should never be automatically added to your bill. It runs as high as $20 per day, and is a good idea if your own car insurance doesn't cover you for rentals.

- [ ] Bodily injury damage: This protection against injuring other drivers is optional but a good idea if your own insurance doesn't cover you.

- [ ] Mileage charge: Sometimes a few cents per mile are added after you exceed a daily or weekly mileage maximum included in the base rate.

- [ ] Local and state taxes.

- [ ] Airport facility and access charges.

- [ ] Refueling charge: To avoid it, fill the car yourself before returning it.

- [ ] Mandatory theft insurance: Required in some overseas countries.

- [ ] One-way service and drop-off charges.

- [ ] Child seats.

- [ ] Additional service fees.

Be sure to book rooms in advance, and try to find a hotel with a swimming pool. A dip in the pool after a long day of driving is a great way to rejuvenate flagging spirits.

You may be able to have food delivered to a highway hotel—a good time- and energy-saving option. Who wants to get back in the car to head out to a restaurant? Order pizza or Chinese and have a party in your room or in a hotel public space. Save leftovers in your cooler for tomorrow's car journey.

Rent a Car or a Van?

There are definite advantages to renting cars or a van for your car trip. If your group is small enough, you may be able to fit everyone in a minivan, and avoid dealing with separate cars. You can save wear and tear on your own car. You may end up with more legroom, you can arrange for luggage and ski racks, and you'll have access to a rental-company-provided 800 number for roadside assistance. Some newer vehicles come equipped with sophisticated dashboard navigational equipment.

TRAVEL BY SHIP

If your family is going the floating-hotel route, you can pretty much just sit back and relax and let the captain do the driving—after you board the ship, that is. Before you board, however, there are a few transportation issues you'll have to figure out, such as how to get to your port of embarkation.

Cruise Tips

If you have to fly into your port of embarkation, you can obtain your airline tickets through a travel agent or through the cruise line's air-sea department. Purchasing an air-sea package through the cruise line guarantees that if your flight is delayed or canceled, the cruise line will make arrangements for you to catch up with the cruise. You may be able to find a cheaper airfare on your own, but you'll have to make your own arrangements if your flight is delayed and you miss the ship. Whatever arrangements you make, be sure to read your cruise line's policy carefully to find out what your responsibilities and entitlements are if a flight delay makes you so late you miss the sailing.

If your extended family is gathering from around the country at a single port, the chances for some kind of flight delay or cancellation are greater for your group. Save yourselves a poor vacation start or at least some worry by arriving at the port the day before the ship sails. Dinner together the night before will add to the excitement and anticipation. Fill out your cruise documents at the hotel, get a good night's rest, and arrive at the vessel on time and relaxed. Board with the first passengers just after noon and enjoy the bon voyage party onboard.

Consider booking a pre- or postcruise tour, which will help you avoid the passenger crush between the cruise ship and the airport. It will also extend your vacation and give you the sense of having two different trips in one—a nice compromise for the landlubbers of your family.

PROS AND CONS OF COACH TOURS

Why stress over planning each day's itinerary when you could be relaxing with family members while sightseeing on an escorted coach tour? Surrender responsibility to your tour guide and driver, sit back, and enjoy the ride.

Coach tours are not for everyone, however, so discuss the pluses and minuses carefully with your family.

On the plus side, a coach tour takes some of the responsibility off your shoulders. You can focus on the scenery and family members while the guide and driver worry about the details. And many escorted tours provide for every aspect of your trip, including airport transportation. Meals are often included as well. And guides are usually quite informative and entertaining.

Depending on the size of your family and budget, you might want to consider booking a private tour. Most motor coaches accommodate 40, but you need a minimum of about 25 to make this a good value compared to buying individual tour tickets. If you have between

30 and 40 on your trip, you actually save by chartering the whole bus.

But some family members prefer independence and privacy. On a bus tour you may be a slave to the clock; you won't have the freedom to change your plans. And keep in mind that most coach tours focus on historic sights; if history is not your family's cup of tea, this is not the right vacation for you.

Hybrid Tours

Some people like escorted tours in limited doses only. In response, tour companies have created hybrid tours that combine both escorted and independent vacation activity. Options include guided days, free nights; escorted country, free city; and hub-and-spoke tours, in which you stay in one central hotel and head out in different directions each day for a different sightseeing excursion.

YOUR OWN DRIVER-GUIDE

If you want the benefits of a knowledgeable escort without having to deal with a coach tour, consider hiring a private driver-guide. The larger your group, the cheaper the cost per person for a driver-guide's service. In most cases you should be able to negotiate a fee per carload of family members. Many guides offer minivan service, which can accommodate about eight family members.

A private driver-guide allows some flexibility for your family. You can hire one for the entire vacation or for one or two days of concentrated sightseeing. If only some family members prefer guided tours, they can make use of a driver-guide's services for a few days of the vacation while other family members sightsee independently.

Finding the Right Guide

Make sure the guide you hire is licensed and certified by the tourist office of the destination you are visiting. This generally means that the guide is a resident of the destination and has studied and passed tests on everything from driving to local history and culture. And, for the record, find out from the tourist office ahead of time if guides receive commissions for leading visitors to certain destinations. Contact potential tour guides by phone or e-mail and ask detailed questions. Ask for references. Make sure you can pay with a credit card.

Discuss your trip before you get in the car with the guide. Come with some firm ideas, but also be prepared to listen to the driver-guide's advice. If he or she strongly recommends a place, it's probably worth giving it a try, although in some cases guides may push you toward places where they make a commission for each visit.

Be prepared to pay for your driver-guide's meals, accommodations, and admission. Gas and tolls are usually included as expenses on the guide's bill. Plan to tip about $5 per person per day.

TRAVEL BY TRAIN

If you want to skip the hassle of flying or driving, consider taking a train to your destination. American trains cross the country, often taking you past stunning scenery. The train ride itself is part of the adventure.

Train seating areas are usually less cramped than cars and airplanes, and it's much easier for family members to get up and move around. Snack cars are convenient, and even with little kids, you never have to stop for a bathroom break.

Some dedicated sightseeing trains offer affordable group rates, including the Durango-Silverton Train in Colorado, and many others. In general, traveling in your own private rail car is an expensive proposition. The average train car can seat just over 60 passengers. If you have that many people in your group, you can reserve seats together on a regular train. To reserve your own dedicated car, there is a per-mile service charge, plus additional fees.

5

Home Away from Home

THE TYPE OF LODGING YOU CHOOSE WILL help set the tone for your vacation. Consider the difference in atmosphere between a business hotel and a chain hotel geared to families, a posh resort and a beach bungalow, or a private rental home and a bed-and-breakfast. Where do you see your extended family having the most fun? If your family relishes fierce debates, avoid places with breakable antiques and marble and brass that seem to demand hushed tones. If privacy is important to your family, consider a rental home. Keep in mind when searching for lodgings that public-space and guest-room decor, staff members, and fellow guests will all influence your behavior and comfort level.

Your destination will likely dictate in part the kind of accommodations you choose. In most popular destinations you will find a range of different properties, which means there's probably something out there to suit your family. Early on in your trip planning sessions discuss and agree upon the ideal facilities, style, and cost of lodgings. When you have an idea of what you want, shop around. Compare properties and ask plenty of questions.

HOTELS, RESORTS, AND B&Bs

What's important to your family on this trip? Recreation? Relaxation? Intimate family gatherings? A little of everything? If yours is an energetic family you may want lots of resort facilities and activities. If you plan on hosting a big family party, a business hotel with meeting rooms might fill the bill. A no-frills chain hotel may be suitable if you plan to spend a lot of time sightseeing and not much at your lodgings.

If you want to hang around together, it might not matter whether there are other people around, and you may want the variety of facilities at a large resort or hotel. Or, if you want to be alone with just your family,

LODGING COMFORTS YOU MAY WANT

- [ ] Adjoining rooms.
- [ ] No-smoking rooms and floors.
- [ ] Room phones.
- [ ] TV in room or public space (with cable, premium channels, and pay-per-view movies).
- [ ] Several restaurants.
- [ ] Room service.
- [ ] Breakfast or all meals included in price.
- [ ] Wheelchair access to all facilities.
- [ ] A swimming pool.
- [ ] Staff-organized sports and recreation.
- [ ] Baby-sitting.
- [ ] Kids' programs (for what ages?).
- [ ] Videogames in rooms or games room.
- [ ] A spa or exercise facilities.
- [ ] A golf course with a teaching pro.
- [ ] Tennis courts.
- [ ] Shuffleboard.
- [ ] Outdoor barbecue or other eating area.
- [ ] Comfortable, attractive meeting rooms.
- [ ] Nightly musical entertainment.
- [ ] Cribs available (fee or free?).
- [ ] Guest laundry, dry-cleaning service.
- [ ] Sightseeing tours available from lobby.
- [ ] Rental cars available nearby.
- [ ] Proximity to airport.
- [ ] Parking lot or covered garage (fee or free?).

some kind of B&B, inn, or small hotel might be in order; while you'd be enjoying a home-like environment, no member of your family would be put into the position of cooking and cleaning up after the whole crew. Choose an inn with a dining room and you've got the perfect formula for a great Thanksgiving weekend together.

Before you start looking at properties, make a list of amenities that are important to your extended family. Rate each amenity on a scale of 1 to 5. Seek out a hotel with all or most of your higher-rated amenities.

Family Friendly or Not?

Some establishments are more family friendly than others. Ask questions before you book. Are adjoining rooms available so children or other relatives can be reached without going through the public hallway? Will the hotel restaurant create a long table or separate dining section that allows your family to sit together at dinner? Are booster seats and high chairs available? Is there a kids' menu? Are cribs available (and does the hostelry have enough of them for everybody in your crew who needs them)? Are children's movies or games available for rental on your guestroom video entertainment system? Is there a video games room? What is there for your teens to do?

Many lodgings proudly cater to families with small children. Others decidedly do not. Ask up front.

EVALUATING CHILDREN'S PROGRAMS

- [ ] What is the ratio of caregivers to children?
- [ ] How are caregivers' backgrounds checked?
- [ ] What are the operating hours and seasons?
- [ ] What ages are accepted?
- [ ] Must kids be toilet-trained?
- [ ] What activities are planned?
- [ ] Are there meals and snacks?
- [ ] How much notice is needed to book?
- [ ] Can you take kids in and out during the day?
- [ ] What's the cost and what's included?

Some properties, more often than not small bed-and-breakfasts, may tell you that they do not accept children under a certain age.

Even a property that welcomes kids with open arms may not be the best bet for your family. Do some research. Discover ahead of time if there's a lobby dress code and whether pool areas have any restrictions against children, including adults-only hours.

Ask questions about a hotel's baby-sitting services and children's programs. Request a printed copy of the children's program guide, which should include a daily schedule of the hour-by-hour activities. Find out what the program offers kids of different ages. Are the 10-year-olds in the same room as the toddlers, or is there a separate activity roster and a separate space?

The Right Price

Local taxes, phone charges, tips for bellhops and maid service, in-room videos, airport shuttle, and other variables can significantly raise initial lodging costs. But with a group of a dozen or more, you can often negotiate so that these extras will be included.

Negotiating Rates

Once you pick a hotel or two or three, you or the family negotiator goes to work. Contact the group sales department or hotel manager. A large group brings a lot of business to a lodging property, so don't be afraid to play hardball. Make sure each hotel knows its competitors are bidding for your business.

Carefully study the "rack rates"—listed brochure rates—and aim for a price one-third lower than that, particularly if you book more than 10 rooms for multiple nights. Seek the equivalent of a free room night for every 10 rooms booked. A travel agent with a booking relationship with the hotel should be able to negotiate this deal.

Also look for other money-saving extras as part of your group rate, such as free breakfast, an afternoon cocktail reception, hotel dining discounts, and free evening entertainment. If there are a bunch of you arriving at staggered times, have a juice-and-snacks setup included. If you plan on booking dinners at hotel restaurants or organizing a party, go for additional discounts for your catering.

Once you agree upon a deal for your group, get it in writing. Study the information carefully and make sure everything you agreed upon with the hotel manager or group sales department is included.

Don't Pay for Extras You Don't Need

The price you pay for your lodging covers much more than just sleeping accommodations. Extra staff services and fancy amenities drive up the price. But why pay for services or amenities your family won't use? Don't spend extra on a resort property with 24-hour room service, cocktail lounges, and a spa if you don't plan on taking advantage of these amenities. Look for a cheaper property with fewer frills and lower prices.

Don't cut out necessities, however. If good housekeeping service and a quality pool are critical, make sure your hotel has them.

Once there, avoid using room phones, which may require you to pay an access charge of $1 or more per call, even for toll-free numbers. Watch out for the minibar, where food and drink charges can be exorbitant. Hotel laundering is also often overpriced. And viewing an in-room movie can cost as much as $15.

Frequent-Guest Awards

Take advantage of relatives' memberships in frequent-guest programs at a hotel chain or frequent flier programs that include hotel awards for mileage redemption. With enough frequent-guest points, you may be able to receive free rooms or room upgrades. Award recipients must be part of the club member's immediate family, but you can reduce the price of everyone's guest room to reflect the savings from the free room.

Hotel policies differ on whether or not you can apply awards to group discounts, but most major chains allow it. If you are a qualifying Hyatt's Gold Passport or Marriott Rewards member, for example, you *can* use frequent-guest points to pay for your room as part of your family's group vacation, so long as there is room availability. Hilton is an exception, though, as reward points may *not* be used to pay for group stays.

Executive Floors

If you're visiting a city over the weekend, consider staying on your hotel's executive floor. A free breakfast is usually included, and you'll likely have access to a lounge your family can use as a common area. Sometimes an evening cocktail reception is included. And you can often check into your hotel right on the floor rather than at the front desk.

On weekdays, when business people are in residence, a chatting family may draw harsh stares from people trying to work, engage in business conversations, or unwind after a long day. Plan accordingly.

Reunion Space

Your hotel may be able to offer an affordable room for your family reunion, especially if you use the party as a negotiating chip to lower your room rates. But before you settle on a hotel space for your party, shop the local area surrounding the hotel for a party site. Ask the local tourism office to recommend places near your hotel. You may find a more affordable place with better food and atmosphere than the hotel party room. If not, you can use the lower price quotes from the nearby venues to negotiate a lower rate.

Coping with Front-Desk Delays

After a long drive or flight, everyone is anxious to drop their bags on the floor and relax in their hotel room. First, however, you've got to check in, a potentially time-consuming operation for a large group. If your group is big enough and family members arrive at staggered times, your hotel might provide a separate check-in desk or an assigned receptionist to make things smoother. If not, arrange for a separate reception room or lobby area for your arriving members. Have juice, coffee, and snacks on hand so that the new arrivals can relax before checking in. Make sure you discuss this when you're negotiating a price.

FAMILY VACATION **RENTALS**

If you're looking for something homier than a hotel, consider a vacation rental. You can rent a house or condo in favorite vacation destinations around the world. On Cape Cod, they're hidden in the woods and along country byways. In the mountains, they cluster around ski resorts—sometimes they're right on the slopes and sometimes perched precipitously above the valley, accessible via a road fraught with hairpin turns. In Tuscany, they're tucked away among the rolling hills, sometimes in the shadow of dramatic cypress trees. In France, you'll find them in Provence, among the lavender fields, among other places. A rental guarantees more privacy and more room, and you won't have to compete with other guests for facilities. A rental property also allows flexibility to arrange parties, barbecues, and games according to your own schedule.

Additionally, your family can save money. Instead of eating every meal in restaurants you can prepare your own food. You'll also avoid paying for hotel services you don't need.

Condominium rentals can prove to be comfortable alternatives to renting a freestanding vacation home.

Condo units are easier to care for and are usually well maintained. Communal facilities include pools, barbecues, parking areas, on-site garbage removal, grounds maintenance, and sometimes even a restaurant. Maid service is more likely to be available than at a private home. Units are private, yet neighbors are nearby and can answer questions. And an on-site rental agent or manager is normally available to help address any questions or problems.

Finding a House

As you would when searching for a hotel, make a list of items that are important to your family. Keep this list in front of you as you explore the options.

Rental Agents

A professional rental agent often has more business skill and can be easier to deal with than the owner of a private vacation home. You'll generally have to pay a slight premium, but using an agent guarantees you certain protections that are worth the extra money. You can sometimes use a credit card with an agency (some vacation homeowners accept only cash), and the agent should be able to help you if any problems arise.

Navigating Rental Web Listings

Many rental companies and rental homeowners advertise their properties on the Web. Although this means you can often view pictures of the home and

RENTAL COMFORTS YOU MAY WANT

- [ ] Deck.
- [ ] Screened porch.
- [ ] Barbecue grill.
- [ ] Maid service.
- [ ] Proximity to beach.
- [ ] Proximity to airport.
- [ ] Oversized beds.
- [ ] Sofa bed.
- [ ] Twin beds.
- [ ] Fans.
- [ ] Air-conditioning (central or in-window).
- [ ] Sports equipment.
- [ ] Swimming pool.
- [ ] Television, with or without cable.
- [ ] VCR or DVD player.
- [ ] Video games.
- [ ] Boardgames, books.
- [ ] Bikes to borrow.
- [ ] Tennis court.
- [ ] Dishwasher.
- [ ] Microwave.
- [ ] Washer/dryer.
- [ ] Linens included.
- [ ] Completely equipped kitchen.
- [ ] Outdoor shower.
- [ ] Lawn and porch furniture.
- [ ] Privacy.
- [ ] Lawn or other grounds.

area and can easily comparison shop, you're also dealing with an element of the unknown. You have no way of knowing if the owner or agent contact is reputable or honest. Check references and do your homework before you send money.

Make sure the site you are studying lists the owner's name, mailing address, phone number, and e-mail address. If there's no contact information but an e-mail address, the owner may not wish to be readily accessible and that could be a problem. If you send an e-mail to a property and don't receive a response in a day or two, it could mean that a property is not being closely managed. Search for dates showing the last time the site was updated; anything that hasn't been updated in the past year means you're probably looking at outdated photos, prices, and information.

Even if you decide that you're not comfortable relying solely on the Web to find a rental property for your family, you can still make good use of the Internet. Checking out Web sites for different rental homes gives you an idea of what to expect to pay in your destination. And if you learn about rental properties through a guidebook or by word of mouth, investigate further through the Web. If you're lucky, you'll discover the property has a site, and since you've already learned elsewhere that it's a good choice, you can study the Web-site information with more confidence.

NOISY NEIGHBORS

Your rental-property owner isn't responsible for the lifestyle of neighbors, but he is responsible for fully informing you about any situation that might negatively affect your vacation. If the next-door neighbor has hostile, barking dogs or renovations in progress, the owner has an obligation to inform you or correct the situation immediately. Ask specific questions before you rent—even about the noise level in the neighborhood—and get confirmation in writing. If you then find the property to have been misrepresented, move elsewhere and stake your legitimate claim to a refund.

Get It in Writing

Before considering a vacation rental, make a list of contract terms and have the owner address in writing each term. Don't send any money, including a down payment, until you have the information in writing. Send any specific questions you have about the property in writing as well, and ask for a written response. Is there a yard? How close are the neighbors? What's the view? Is there construction going on in the neighborhood? Confirm your understanding of the answers, and keep this documentation with your financial records.

As a rule, large rental companies that rent vacation units in resort communities do not charge an extra cleanup fee for when you leave the property. For a week's vacation, cleaning fees are included. But when you rent an individual home or condo from a private owner, the owners do tend to charge a cleanup fee, ranging from $75 for a condo to up to $250 for a full-size house. Individual owners may also allow you to clean the rental yourself. Ask about your owner's policy, and confirm the arrangements in writing.

Payment Arrangements

Most rental owners require you to provide a 10% to 15% nonrefundable down payment to reserve dates you have planned for your vacation. The full rental and damage deposit is usually due about two months before your arrival. Paying with a credit card ensures some protection, but this is not always an option if you deal directly with the owner as opposed to a rental agent. Obtain prompt receipts for all payments as well as signed copies of the rental agreements. Know how and when your deposit will be returned.

Local Contact

Before finalizing your rental plans ask the owner for a local contact whom you can notify in case of a problem or emergency during your stay. If no contact is available, find out where the owner will be during your vacation period and agree on times when you can contact him or her by phone with questions or

WHAT TO NOTE IN RENTAL PAPERWORK

- [ ] Arrival and departure dates.
- [ ] Rental fee and payment schedule.
- [ ] State of property on arrival: fully cleaned, and supplied with fresh linens and bedding.
- [ ] Bathrooms are in working order.
- [ ] Kitchen contains pots and pans, utensils, plates, glasses, and appliances that work.
- [ ] Extra towels, blankets, sheets, and pillowcases are available.
- [ ] Heat or air-conditioning that works.
- [ ] Owner or agent meets you on arrival day to jointly note any damage predating your arrival.
- [ ] Damage deposit and a deadline for its return ($200 and up).
- [ ] Maid service included or extra.
- [ ] Payment terms for use of telephone.
- [ ] Televisions work (also cable and VCR or DVD player, if present).
- [ ] Use of owner's property: barbecue, bicycles, sports equipment.
- [ ] Garbage disposal arrangements: you dump or they pick up.
- [ ] Cleaning responsibilities on departure—what to do with unused food.

concerns. Be wary if a rental owner refuses to provide a contact or remain in touch during your stay.

On Vacation: Cleanup and Kitchen Duties

Don't let the burden of cleaning and cooking fall solely on the shoulders of a few people. Plan to share these duties. If your group is small enough, you might want to divide into two squads, one for cooking and one for cleaning up after meals. Have the squads alternate duties each night.

Another idea is to assign couples or small groups to cook for each night of your vacation. Let family members know the cooking schedule in advance, before you even leave for your trip, so they can plan ahead and maybe bring a favorite recipe. Plan a catered dinner for your farewell party. Rotate family members on post-dining cleanup duty as well.

Individuals and family groups should be responsible for cleaning their own sleeping areas, and you should all share responsibility for cleaning communal spaces. Set aside some time just before you leave to straighten up the rental property.

If you don't think your family can handle cleaning and cooking duties, consider hiring a housekeeping service (or inviting your own housekeeper to join you). Or ask the on-site manager at a rental community

When my mother, three adult brothers and sisters, and our eight children gather for our annual family vacation, we spread out in a six-bedroom house within walking distance of a gorgeous beach. We've worked out a good system for sharing the expense and work of mealtimes. Everyone brings groceries and as the week goes on, we shop as needed and keep all our receipts. The last morning we add them up and then divide by the number of family units. (Grandma is our guest and doesn't have to contribute.) That way we don't have to be constantly dealing with

TRAVEL LOG money during the reunion. As for cooking, we go out the first night and then form two-person teams to make dinner each night. The teams aren't necessarily spouses or parent and child, which makes it more fun as in-laws or cousins work on a project together and get to know each other in whole new ways. Breakfast is usually up to the individual, unless someone feels like making pancakes for everyone. Two sisters have a great, assembly line picnic-making system down pat, and so they always bring lunch to the beach for everyone. All in all, we eat well and no one feels overworked.

—Liana R., Emeryville, California

for recommendations on hiring local help, or contact the local tourist office, which should maintain a listing of registered services. Obtain and check references before hiring anyone.

CRUISE ACCOMMODATIONS

Your family's comfort depends on getting the accommodations right on a cruise ship. And with so many different cabin categories—outside and inside cabins, cabins with full views and cabins with partially obstructed views, cabins with full bathtubs and cabins with shower stalls—you'll need to think carefully about your family's requirements.

Choosing Cabins

Obtain a deck map of the ship you are considering and have your family study it carefully before deciding what type of cabins to reserve. Higher decks and midship cabins usually provide smoother sailing in rough seas and are, accordingly, more expensive.

Note the proximity of cabin areas to dining rooms, nightclubs, theaters, stairwells, and the aft (rear) of the ship near engine-room bulkheads—all of which can be noisy.

When selecting cabins, make it clear to the cruise sales department or your travel agent that your family will not accept cabins in noisy areas. It's sometimes difficult to learn cabin assignments in advance. Once you get cruise documents with cabin numbers, check your map locations and have an agent or cruise representative confirm that your cabins are away from the noise. If not, get on the phone at once to ask for reassignments. Travel agents who specialize in selling cruises and have ties to cruise lines can help you reserve specific cabin numbers in advance.

Also find out how the cruise line charges single travelers. Sometimes there are single supplements, and the solo travelers in your family may decide to gang up— or you may decide to choose another ship.

Family members with mobility problems should select a cabin near an elevator or stairway midship. Be careful not to book a cabin with upper and lower berths.

If you are bringing a baby, request the crib in advance and make sure the cabin you choose is big enough to accommodate it.

Outside and Inside

Within your extended family, households with children can save money by renting pairs of outside cabins opposite inside cabins (without windows) rather than side-by-side outside cabins. The children can sleep in the cheaper interior cabins, while the adults enjoy a window. An outside cabin with a private balcony drives up the price, but it affords an outdoor "living room" where family members can gather. If you have several households in your extended families, consider ordering a block of outside-inside combinations.

6

The Gang's All Here

THE CAST OF CHARACTERS IS IN PLACE, the scene is set, and anticipation is high for your production—The Whole-Entire-Family Vacation. The best way to make sure your production garners rave reviews is to plan your vacation activities with the same care you put into planning the budget, location, lodgings, and transportation. Designate an entertainment director to organize events and serve as the go-to person for questions related to activities and festivities. After discussion with the rest of the family, the entertainment director should arrange for any major activities that require reservations, such as family parties, sporting events, and tours. For large groups, instruct the entertainment director to give each family member a printed itinerary that highlights prearranged activities and free time. The entertainment director should also bring (or arrange for others to bring) any sporting equipment, games, or other diversions integral to your fun.

That's not to say you should micromanage. Spontaneity is part of any vacation, and you want to give yourself room to go with the flow once you get there. But have some firm ideas about what you'll be doing with your days and evenings, with backup plans just in case. Gauge your family's ability to create its own entertainment or its need to be entertained, and plan accordingly.

ALL TOGETHER NOW

Remember why you're taking this trip in the first place? To spend time with your extended family in a vacation setting.

To make sure that happens, plan group activities that allow you to interact, bond, have fun, and revive relationships with relatives you haven't seen in a while. Charades and golf do more for family togetherness than watching videos (unless, of course, yours is a family of passionate movie critics bent on discussing films). Leave free time for people to just sit around and talk, but have some concrete ideas in mind for family activities as well.

If you're with a very large family group or at a reunion, you may want to start off the first few events and days with name tags. Though they may elicit groans from some family members, they can spare you the embarrassment of forgetting your distant in-law's or third cousin's name.

How to Decide on Activities Once You Arrive

Let dinner be the time for your family to discuss how to spend each coming day for which you haven't prearranged an event. Ask each family member to bring one or two ideas for group activities to the table, and discuss the ideas aloud. If you can't reach a consensus, consider breaking up into groups to pursue different activities. Remember, you can all get together again at lunch and dinner.

Going Your Own Way

Don't make a fuss if a family member wants to pursue his or her own agenda for a day. Every minute doesn't have to be "family time," and letting someone

GET CREATIVE WITH ACTIVITIES

- ☐ Go for an early morning balloon ride.
- ☐ Take a walk on the beach at dawn.
- ☐ Go to a church with good music.
- ☐ Watch a horse show.
- ☐ Take a group cooking class.
- ☐ Schedule a guided hike.
- ☐ Visit a restoration village.
- ☐ Explore a nature preserve.
- ☐ Scuba dive or snorkel.
- ☐ Rent bikes.
- ☐ Sign up for sailing or surfing lessons.
- ☐ Go to an auction or antiques market.

drop out for a day or two will likely keep the peace, especially if there are family tensions. Early on in your planning meetings let everyone know this is okay.

Your Backup Plan

Even the best-laid plans sometimes fall apart. You've scheduled boat trips and picnics for your beach vacation, but when you get there it rains nonstop for five days. Or little Mickey, who has always loved toy ships, discovers that being on a real one for the day makes him feel sick.

Everyone wants to have a good time on this trip, and will work toward that goal. But you should still have backup ideas in case something goes wrong. Before you leave home, book tickets to an indoor event or a show that you can enjoy rain or shine. Or find out ahead of time where the best shopping areas are in your destination, just in case. If possible, bring along games you can play indoors in case of rain or as a break from sightseeing. Some resorts have board games on hand for guest use. On a rainy night, tell childhood stories or pretend you're having a slumber party. Order an in-room movie the whole family can watch in your hotel room. Don't concern yourself too much that these are all things you can do at home: the point is to be together, and to create some fun when the vacation is faltering.

If you have friends or relatives who live in the destination, consider contacting them before the trip to arrange a get-together once you arrive. This may provide a needed break from vacation mode, and it's possible your friends or relatives can suggest other amusements in the area if your plans start to unravel.

You Can't Please Everyone

Keep your expectations realistic. If you plan well and take at least part of each family branch's suggestions into account, you have a good chance of pleasing the majority of the members. There may be a few

SAMPLE REUNION WEEKEND

Friday

- ☐ 2 PM to 6 PM: Guests arrive. Registration.
- ☐ 7 PM to 10 PM: Welcome reception and buffet meal.
- ☐ 10 PM: Individual family groups host dessert and coffee in their rooms.

Saturday

- ☐ 8 AM to 10 AM: Buffet breakfasts.
- ☐ 10 AM to 1 PM: Free time.
- ☐ 1 PM to 3 PM: Family barbecue.
- ☐ 3 PM to 4:30 PM: Family softball or soccer.
- ☐ 4:30 PM to 8 PM: Free time.
- ☐ 8 PM to midnight: Gala family-reunion party with live music, meal service, open bar. Disposable cameras and address books on each table. Open seating.

Sunday

- ☐ 8 AM to 10 AM: Continental breakfast.
- ☐ 10 AM to noon: Free time.
- ☐ Noon to 2 PM: Family buffet brunch.
- ☐ 2 PM to 7 PM: Free time. Swim meet and family games.
- ☐ 7 PM to 10 PM: Casual pasta party or clambake. Distribute reunion mementos.

Monday

- ☐ 7 AM to 10 AM: Breakfast and good-byes.

unhappy attendees who grumble over a meal or an activity. Tune them out and search out instead the people with smiles on their faces. And remember, you accomplished the main goal of the reunion: bringing your extended family together. Don't be surprised if they ask you to plan the next one.

By the Beach or in the Country

If your family is heading to the beach, a lakeside cottage, or a rural country house, you probably won't have much sightseeing planned. Use your time for family-focused activities that allow you to enjoy your natural surroundings. Schedule barbecues and a picnic dinner under the stars. Gather around a campfire. Look for a music festival, a local fair, or for fireworks if you're vacationing around the Fourth of July. Fly a kite or two. Rent or charter a boat.

Family Tournaments

Schedule a game of softball, beach volleyball, or kickball. If your crowd is large, set up several teams and make it a tournament. If you've rented a house with its own pool or you're staying at a hotel with a pool (you may be able to reserve the pool for your exclusive use for a few hours) pencil in a day of water Olympics. Plan swimming and nonswimming events of all levels with different family teams. You might have a relay race with team members paddling a raft by hand from one end of the pool to the other. Or try dog-paddle races or parent-child relays (two parents and two kids on a team). If you have access to kickboards, you can race freestyle with kickboards under your stomach or backstroke with the kickboard under your head. If your family includes many children, have the biggest member of each team sit in a rubber inner tube at the shallow end of the pool. Two children from each team must push their team's tube across the pool and back. The first team to reach the wall wins.

If you're not much for swimming, stage a field day with games and relays, with starting points and end points marked by a cone or other item set up about 25 yards away. One favorite is an egg-on-spoon relay, where your team has to carry an egg on a spoon to the cone and back without dropping it. But there are many variations. Give each team a cup, and put a bucket full of water near the cone and an empty bucket at the starting point; see which team ends up with the most water in the bucket when each team member has made one run.

Don't forget about those old summer-camp favorites: sack races, three-legged races, tug-of-wars, red light/green light, and capture the flag. Not to mention hide and seek, duck-duck-goose, and musical chairs.

Choose up or assign color teams, and have everyone wear something in his or her team colors. Lollipops as prizes generate extra enthusiasm for these events among youngsters.

Scavenger hunts are fun for a group as well. Ask the kids to get together to create one for the adults, if you run out of time to plan it in advance.

Gone Fishing

On a chartered fishing boat, with crew, even family members who don't want to fish can just sit back and enjoy the boat. Fill a cooler with cold drinks and snacks. Set aside a reward for the person who reels in the most or biggest fish.

Prices vary by location and boat, but usually run several hundred dollars per day or half-day. Also, when booking the boat, ask if there are any shaded areas so that people can take a break from the sun. Look for a deal that includes poles, bait and tackle, and basic instruction. You can often even arrange for the crew to clean your fish.

Rainy Days

If the great outdoors is the theme of your vacation and the weather isn't cooperating, you'll have to rely on each other to keep the fun alive. A rainy day can be a great chance to spend family time together. Encourage the entertainment director to come up with ideas for rainy-day fun before you leave for your vacation. Bring board games and cards, or call ahead to your hotel to see if they keep games on hand for guest use. Try charades. Play an innocuous version of spin the bottle in which each person chosen has to perform before the group—a song, a poem, a story, a dance, or whatever strikes her fancy.

Kids and family members who like arts and crafts can get creative during poor weather. If you're staying near a beach and you see bad weather coming, gather shells and driftwood on the shore before the downpour begins. Buy cord, glue, any other materials to make a project—a seashell sculpture, wind chimes, or the like. Whatever you do, don't turn on the TV.

Cruises

Familiarize yourselves with the ports of call beforehand. Check out your cruise line's shore excursions pamphlet. Decide among yourselves for each port

> **TRAVEL LOG**
>
> A few years ago when our family rented a beach cottage for a summer week, it rained and the temperature was cool almost every day. We discovered a stable in the neighborhood where you could ride the trails in light rain. We donned rain gear and hats and, in gray weather and slight drizzle, were able to go riding for a few hours on three different days. The loudest cheer of our vacation came one day when we rode down to the beach and the sun actually came out for 10 minutes! We didn't get any decent beach days, but those horses saved our vacation.
>
> —*Brendan P., Alexandria, Virginia*

whether you're going to book a private guide through a travel agent before you leave, take part in the ship's guided tour, or explore the port on your own. You may want to do a combination: arrange for a private tour for one or two ports ahead of time and leave your options open for other ports.

Most cruise lines slide a newsletter for the following day's activities, including shore excursions, under the door while you're at dinner. Have all family members scan the list and discuss what you plan on doing for the coming day. Again, be flexible about breaking up into different groups.

Some of your cruise-ship days will be spent entirely at sea, with no ports of call, but ships are loaded with activities and facilities—from expansive sundecks and multiple swimming pools to arcades and virtual-reality centers to shops and miniature golf courses. When booking your cruise, you can also arrange for special events for your family, such as karaoke, family bingo night, or pool games.

The Talent Contest

Many cruise ships host guest talent nights. Here's your family's big chance. Prepare a favorite song. Select a lead singer, backup singers, and a dance line. Set a theme, create costumes, and rehearse. Be goofy and have fun. You may not score a recording contract, but you will certainly achieve fame among your fellow passengers for a day or two. Obtain a recording or video of your song if possible.

City Time

Don't overschedule family events in big cities. Rather than staying in a close-knit group for your entire city vacation, break into small clusters to explore different areas of interest. The city will hold a different kind of appeal for each family member. Let arts lovers seek out performances and galleries. Send sports fans out to see a game. Shoppers may have bargain hunting on their minds.

Do schedule rendezvous times and places as well. Meet at a designated spot for breakfast, lunch, or dinner so that you can all talk about what you've been doing. Be sure to plan big family parties and dinners as trip highlights.

With a large group, book certain activities in advance, such as city tours, theater and sporting events, and group dinners.

Pre-Reserve Meals and Shows

The best theater and concert tickets usually require reservations months in advance. With a group of 20 people or more, you can often reserve a block of seats at a group discount. To qualify for discounts at Broadway shows in New York City, which are generally 10% off for performances Monday through Thursday, you usually have to order tickets two to three months in advance. You may not be able to get a discount for the most popular shows, but some long-running favorites sell half-price tickets to groups. No payment is required to reserve a block of tickets, but you must pay 30 days before the performance. Up until you pay you can change your dates without penalty; once you pay, no refunds or changes are allowed.

If you arrive at a restaurant without a reservation in a big group for lunch between noon and 2, or dinner between 6 and 8, be prepared to wait to be seated—

particularly for lunch on a weekday or for dinner on a Friday or Saturday night. Even if you have a reservation you may end up waiting a while. To avoid delays, make a reservation for a late lunch, at 2:30 or so, or an early dinner, at 5:30.

Ballpark Discounts

If your large family group plans on attending a sporting event, contact the team's group sales department rather than going through the box office. A group of about 12 or more usually qualifies for discount tickets and extras such as discount coupons for stadium merchandise. If you have 30 or more, inquire well ahead about the possibility of renting a skybox. Companies usually reserve these 50-seat spaces for a full season, but onetime rentals may be available on certain dates. They have indoor and outdoor seating, TV monitors inside, a kitchen and bar, and even catering for an additional charge.

Shop til You Drop—Together

You and your family may be picking up souvenirs and clothing as you visit gift shops at each attraction, but you may also want to dedicate a day to shopping. Look for items and crafts unique to the area you're visiting. Or use the opportunity to pick up family holiday or birthday gifts—here's your chance to pull Aunt Mimi aside and ask her to help you find Uncle Bert a birthday gift. Or if you see your mother eyeing a sweater or piece of jewelry, buy it to surprise her for Mother's Day. Break up into groups and gather again for lunch.

Walking Tours

In just about every major city your family can join a literary, historical, architectural, or other theme walking tour (on themes ranging from celebrity hangouts to ghostly haunts). Some tours take place only on weekends; others are available on weekdays as well. These tours are a great way to learn about the city you're visiting, and guides are often energetic and entertaining. You can even hire a private guide to tailor a walk to your family's interests.

Picnic in the Park

Just because you're in a big city doesn't mean you can't get some fresh air. Plan a picnic for your family. Stop at a street market for fresh bread, cheese and fruit, and salads; pack a blanket and a Frisbee; and head for a local park. Enjoy people-watching, go for a jog, take a walk, play a game, catch up, and plan your next adventure.

THE CHILDREN'S HOURS

If your extended family includes many children, you'll likely be doing quite a few group activities together. And though you'll probably find lots to do to keep family members of all ages happy, the adults and children in your family might all enjoy some time apart. Let kids spend time with other children, either within your family or at children's clubs, and let the adults enjoy some kids-free time.

Kids on Their Own

Make sure other responsible adults in your family will be around to watch your children when they're not with an organized program and when you can't be there. When the kids plan their own activities, especially with new friends, give them some space. This is a good opportunity for them to forge friendships with distant relatives of their own age.

Pizza Party

Order a few pies, leave an adult or two behind to supervise, and let the kids bond. Rent a video, plan an outdoor sporting activity, or organize a treasure hunt as part of the party. Meanwhile the rest of the adults in the family can have a quiet dinner. And remember to reward the adults who stayed behind to supervise.

Night Owls

Once kids turn 13 or so, many shun the morning like vampires, preferring instead to stay up late and do their thing, then sleep in the next day. You don't want your little night owls missing out on family activities every day, but be flexible—slumber parties are part of the bonding process.

The Essential Movie Break

After several days of active travel and unfamiliar surroundings, a movie provides a nice break. If you can't all agree on one, break up into a couple of groups and see different shows at a multiplex. If there are none near you, see if your hotel rents out VCRs and videos.

Keep a Scrapbook

Let the children create a scrapbook of their vacation. They can collect postcards, brochures, candy wrappers, ticket stubs, or other ephemera; draw pictures of their favorite places; and write descriptions of what they have seen. Several children can even team up to create a trip scrapbook for the whole group. Leave space to paste in photographs once you're back at home.

Tired Feet

It can happen anywhere—at an amusement park, a zoo, a mall. After a few hours of sightseeing the tired-feet syndrome kicks in. It doesn't affect children only, but they're the ones who will probably complain the loudest. When you're out exploring or shopping, pick clusters of attractions in a small area to minimize walking. Keep sightseeing down to 90 minutes at a stretch. Plan a midmorning break, an early lunch, and tea in late afternoon, the cranky hour. A clean pair of socks is surprisingly refreshing and may keep you going until it's time to head back to the hotel for a swim, a snack, or a movie.

With Your Grandkids

If you spend the day at the pool with the children while the parents head off for a hike, you will not only get a chance to catch up with your grandkids, but you'll also give their parents a break that they'll appreciate for days to come.

Vacationing with your grandchildren can put you in closer continuous contact with them than you've ever had before. But pace yourself, and do plan some breaks and rest for yourself.

Grandchild Prime Time

Mornings after breakfast may be the best time for grandparent-grandchildren activities—a trip to the zoo, theme park, a museum, or a show. Wind down with lunch and return them to their parents. Or join the rest of your family for a group activity.

Sightseeing

Limit sightseeing stops to one, two, or at most three places. Build plenty of breaks into your schedule. Find out in advance if, say, a children's museum has guided tours or special events, and reserve your place. One good city strategy is to schedule something lively in the morning like a visit to an interactive science museum, an escorted walking tour, or a trip to a zoo. After lunch, plan a more leisurely activity. Go on a sightseeing boat tour, take in a matinee, or try a hop-on, hop-off bus

TRAVEL LOG

I've discovered my five-year-old granddaughter loves going to a formal tea service when we visit the city. She puts on her nicest party dress and we spend the day sightseeing. I make a reservation in a town house restaurant or a hotel reception room with good people-watching. We dine at an elegantly set table with gleaming silverware, and the waiters usually make a fuss over her. She requests, and receives, her milk in the same fine china in which the tea is served. We munch on finger sandwiches and scones and discuss our day. By the time the biscuits, éclairs, and chocolate-dipped strawberries arrive, my granddaughter is in heaven. It's a wonderful experience.

—*Maureen S., Huntington, New York*

---

tour that allows you to disembark at an attraction and get back on at the same or another location.

Cruise Shows

On board ship, while your adult children try their luck in the casino or nightclub after dinner, take the kids to an early performance of a stage show. Most are geared to family audiences. Discuss the idea with your grandchildren to make sure the production interests them. Disney Cruise Line shows star favored Disney characters, while many other cruise lines stage scenes from popular musicals like *Cats* or *Phantom of the Opera*. Magic shows, comedy routines, and variety shows are other possibilities.

THE PARTY'S OVER: TIME TO LEAVE

All good things, including your extended-family vacation, must come to an end. And believe it or not, you even need to plan for the end of your vacation. The more smoothly the last days of your trip go, the easier it will be for everyone to ease out of holiday mode back into the real world.

Plan a big end-of-the-trip bash—not necessarily on the very last evening of the trip.

Make Your Memories Last

Pass around a comments book, the kind used at small hotels and bed-and-breakfasts, for family members to sign, write notes, and leave their contact information. (You want to stay in touch, now that you've gone to all the trouble to get together.) When you get home, make copies of the comment pages and send them to family members along with some favorite photographs to help preserve everyone's memories. Don't leave without taking a group photo. If you have a big group, create a who's-who caption on the back side of the photo. Get copies made for everyone.

Fond Farewells

Allow plenty of time for your family to say their good-byes before the mad rush to the airport or the drive back home. A midday departure will allow you to eat breakfast, exchange information, and make

YOUR LAST BASH TOGETHER

Schedule your farewell party on the evening before the last night of vacation. No one wants to go home tired, with indigestion or a headache from having partied to hard or stayed up too late. Let the final evening entail an early meal, with time to pack later on and plan on a nice breakfast the next day. Most of the family will have recovered from the big party in time for departure. And the children will be more rested and easier for parents to handle on the homeward journey.

You might consider designating one member of your group to videotape your party. The camera operator's assistant can do a video interview of each participant. What was their favorite part of the vacation, you might ask. Or ask everyone to reminisce on camera. Then you can make copies of the tape (or the digital file) and distribute them to every household.

The Party's Over: Time to Leave **171**

future plans. If you've scheduled early morning departures, make dinner the night before the time to say good-bye.

If certain staff members at your destination have played a big role in your family vacation—perhaps the waitstaff that served you for the duration of your cruise, for example, or a favorite kid's club counselor—be sure to thank them properly on your final evening. A nice touch, in addition to a good tip, is to have your children or grandchildren thank the staff personally, or even to make a card. Remember to take some photographs of the children with the staff as souvenirs.

Plan for Future Events

If your trip went smoothly and you think your family might be up for another vacation together, introduce the idea at one of your last meals. Discuss possible destinations and dates, without going into detail. The idea is not to start planning immediately but to simply ascertain whether most of you are interested in doing this again. Come up with ways the vacation could be even better and jot down ideas.

Or introduce the possibility of a single-day gathering in the near future. Make it a postvacation party, where you can share photographs and relive your trip.

Grab-Bag Farewell Gifts

At the start of the trip, place each family member's name on a slip of paper in a hat. Let family members draw a name and buy a destination-related farewell gift for that person by the end of the trip to distribute at the farewell party. Set a price limit. A shell necklace from a tropical island, logo-wear from a cruise ship, or a book on your destination all serve as great mementos of the trip.

Going Home Happy

The end of any vacation, particularly a good one, can be disappointing. Soon you'll be back at work or school. And the trip home can be trying.

Think positive. Don't spend going-home day dwelling on what went wrong. Avoid talking about family members in a negative light, especially around children. Discussing the disappointing party, a hotel problem, or a bad meal as you head home only makes them seem worse and may detract from other family members' sense of enjoyment. Give your trip the benefit of time and distance before making judgments. Hopefully the family will agree that the vacation, despite the occasional mishap, was a positive experience well worth sharing.

Focus on the positive. Discuss your favorite vacation experience, place, game, and meal during your flight or drive.

For Kids

Encourage children to draw pictures of highlights. You can even make a game of it: have family members try to guess what each picture represents. Collect the pictures for the family scrapbook.

Give each school-age child a small address book into which he or she can copy the names and addresses of distant family members and new friends. Encourage the children to write letters once they return home, or even on the flight home.

A Photo Exchange and Scrapbook

Ask your relatives to choose three or four of their favorite vacation photographs, with the date and setting marked on the back, and send them to you or someone in your family who's computer-savvy to scan onto a computer. Print up pages of the best photographs and send a copy to each family group. This is an easy, inexpensive way to share memories.

Alternatively, create a trip Web site.

Or get together with a few family members or your own immediate family and create a scrapbook of photographs and other mementos from your trip. Collect your photos and those from your fellow family travelers and arrange them by destination or family group. If you have kids, let them help you choose the final photos and write captions. Add color to your scrapbook. Include a menu from the family party or brochures from places you stayed, ate, and visited. Paste in postcards. And bring the finished product to your next family gathering.

It may just become the inspiration for your next vacation together.

Resources

FODOR'S RESOURCES

Fodors.com
This is a great place to begin planning your family vacation, with its profiles of many worthy destinations and many links. If you don't find what you're looking for, you can post questions in the Forums section and, usually, get a quick answer from people who have been there and done exactly what you're proposing.

Guidebooks and References
A good travel guide gives you an unbiased, inside story on where to sleep and eat, what to see and do, and how to get around in destinations you might want to visit.

Fodor's Escapes
If your family's choice is a get-away-from-it-all adventure, check out these collections of unique experiences in paradise destinations from Tuscany and Provence to Morocco and Hawaii.

Fodor's Gold Guides
Fodor's flagship series of guidebooks, covering destinations around the world. Each volume includes detailed information on hundreds of places to stay, eat, and explore.

Fodor's Pocket Guides
Quick and easy guides to major cities.

AIR TRAVEL

Aviation Consumer Protection Division
www.dot.gov/airconsumer
U.S. Department of Transportation
400 Seventh St., SW
Washington, DC 20590
202/366-2220

Federal Aviation Administration
www.faa.gov
800 Independence Ave., SW
Washington, DC 20591
202/366-4000
Current information on airport procedures, airline regulations.

Consolidators

United States Air Consolidators Association
www.usaca.com
926 L St.
Sacramento, CA 95814
916/441-4166

United States Tour Operators Association
www.ustoa.com
275 Madison Ave., Ste. 2014
New York, NY 10016
212/599-6599

Has some consolidators among its members.

Air by Pleasant
www.airbypleasant.com
4025 Camino del Rio S, Ste. 210
San Diego, CA 92108
800/877-8111

D-FW Tours
www.dfwtours.com
7616 LBJ Freeway, Ste. 524
Dallas, TX 75251
800/527-2589

GTI Consolidators
515 E. 8th St.
Holland, MI 49423
800/829-8234

Pacific Gateway
320 SW Stark St., Ste. 315
Portland, OR 97204
800/777-8369
www.pacificgateway.com

Airport-Transfer Information

SuperShuttle
www.supershuttle.com
800/622-2089
Airport car and van service in 15 cities.

Frequent Flier Programs

www.FrequentFlier.com
Tips and updates, plus airport links, boards, history, and details on programs.

Inside Flyer
www.webflyer.com
800/209-2870
Definitive source of everything to know about frequent travel programs.

ARTS ACTIVITIES

Group Sales Box Office
www.bestofbroadway.com
226 W. 47th St.
New York, NY 10036
800/223-7565

League of Broadway Producers
www.broadway.org
226 W. 47th St.
New York, NY 10036
212/764-1122
Links to Broadway shows and a Live Broadway for Kids Club.

Society of London Theatre
www.officiallondontheatre.co.uk
32 Rose St.
London WC2E 9ET
(011)207/557–6700 in Britain
Comprehensive source of British show tickets and information.

Theater Direct International
www.broadwaydirect.com
1650 Broadway, Ste. 910
New York, NY 10019
800/334-8457
Tickets to Broadway and London shows.

BEACHES

Laboratory For Coastal Research
www.topbeaches.com
Florida International University
Miami, FL 33199
Listings and reviews of America's most pollution-free, beautiful beaches.

BOAT CHARTERS

Bareboat Sailing Charters
www.bareboatsailing.com
6 Maplewood Rd.
Old Saybrook, CT 06475
800/661-4013

Horizon Yacht Charters
www.horizonyachtcharters.com
Box 11156
St. Thomas, USVI 00801
877/494-8787
With crew or without.

Newport Boat Show
www.newportboatshow.com
Newport Yachting Center
Newport, RI 02840
America's largest boat show (mid-Sept.), full of charter options.

CAMPING AND HIKING

About.com
www.camping.about.com
Information and links to campgrounds nationwide.

Canada Camper
www.canada-camper.com
4431 Vanguard Rd.
Richmond, BC V6X 2P6
Canada
604/270-1833
Motor home rentals across North America.

Cruise America
www.cruiseamerica.com
11 W. Hampton Ave.
Mesa, AZ 85210
480/464-7300
A U.S. camper-rental network.

Gorp
www.gorp.com
The ultimate outdoors lover's Web site, with profiles of major parks and forests, suggested hikes, links, and more.

Kampgrounds of America
www.koa.com
Box 30558
Billings, MT 59114
406/248-7444

National Forest Service
www.fs.fed.us
U.S. Department of Agriculture
201 14th Street, SW
Washington, DC 20250

National Park Foundation
www.nationalparks.org
11 Dupont Circle, NW, 6th floor
Washington, DC 20036
202/238-4200
Nonprofit partner of the National Park Services; Web site sells National Parks Pass and has links.

National Park Service
www.nps.gov
1849 C Street NW
Washington, DC 20240
202/208-6843
The National Park Service site lists addresses of regional offices and has official information and links for all parks.

U.S. National Parks Net
www.us-national-parks.net
A well-organized independent Web site with links to many parks; not affiliated with the Park Service.

CANOEING AND RAFTING

America Outdoors
www.americaoutdoors.org
Box 10847
Knoxville, TN 37939
865/558-3595
The national association of outfitters and guides can provide information on member outfitters.

American Canoe Association
www.acanet.org
7432 Alban Station Blvd., Ste. B232
Springfield, VA 22150
703/451-0141
Information on guided tours and instruction in all paddle sports.

Outfitters

Alaska Discovery
www.akdiscovery.com
5310 Glacier Hwy.
Juneau, AK 99801
800/586-1911

Dvorak's Kayak and Rafting Expeditions
www.dvorakexpeditions.com
17921 US Hwy. 285
Nathrop, CO 81236
719/539-6851, 800/824-3795

Echo: The Wilderness Company
www.echotrips.com
6529 Telegraph Ave.
Oakland, CA 94609-1113
510/652-1600, 800/652-3246

Grand Canyon Expeditions
www.gcex.com
Box 0
Kanab, UT 84741
435/644-2691, 800/544-2691

Hatch River Expeditions
www.hatchriver.com
Box 1150
Vernal, UT 84078
435/789-4316, 800/342-8243

Hughes River Expeditions
www.hughesriver.com
Box 217
Cambridge, ID 83610
208/257-3477, 800/262-1882

Laughing Heart Adventures
www.pcweb.net/laughingheart/adventures
Box 669
Willow Creek, CA 95573
530/629-3516, 888/271-6235

Nantahala Outdoor Center
www.noc.com
13077 Hwy. 19 West
Bryson City, NC 28713
828/488-2175, 800/232-7238

O.A.R.S.
www.oars.com
Box 67
Angels Camp, CA 95222
209/736-4677, 800/346-6277

Rocky Mountain River Tours
www.rafttrips.com
Box 8596
Boise, ID 83707
208/345-2400, 208/756-4808 summer

Sundance River Center
www.sundanceriver.com
344 Thornridge La.
Merlin, OR 97532
541/479-8508, 888/777-7557

CAR RENTALS

Auto Europe
www.autoeurope.com
39 Commercial St.
Box 7006
Portland, ME 04112
207/842-2000, 888/223-5555
U.S.-based European rentals.

Avis
www.avis.com
800/452-1534

Free advance travel information and messaging service in Europe.

Budget
www.budget.com
800/527-0700

Dollar
www.dollar.com
800/800-4000

Hertz
www.hertz.com
800/654-3131

Kemwel Auto
www.kemwel.com
800/678-0678
Discounted prepaid rental programs for Europe.

National
www.national.com
800/227-7368

CRUISE TRAVEL

Cruise Agencies

National Association of Cruise Oriented Agencies
www.nacoaonline.com/contact.html
7600 Red Rd.
Miami, FL 33143
305/663-5626
An association that numbers many of the country's cruise specialist agencies among its members.

Cruise Lines

Carnival Cruise Lines
www.carnival.com
800/438-6744

Celebrity Cruises
www.celebritycruises.com
800/437-3111

Cruise Lines International Association
www.cruising.org
500 Fifth Ave., Ste. 1407
New York, NY 10110
212/921-4711
Information on 25 member lines.

Delta Queen Steamboat Co.
www.amcv.com
Robin Street Wharf
1380 Port of New Orleans Pl.
New Orleans, LA 70130
504/586-0631
Spring to fall cruises on the National Historic Landmark paddlewheeler *Delta Queen*.

Disney Cruise Line
www.disneycruise.com
800/939-2784

Norwegian Cruise Line
www.ncl.com
800/327-7030

Princess Cruises
www.princesscruises.com
800/774-6237

Royal Caribbean International
www.royalcaribbean.com
800/327-6700

Star Cruises
www.starcruises.com
305/436-4694
Affiliated with Norwegian Cruise Line. Luxury Southeast Asian sailings.

Ports

Greater Fort Lauderdale Convention and Visitors Bureau
www.sunny.org
1850 Eller Dr., Ste. 303
Fort Lauderdale, FL 33316
954/765-4466
South Florida's Port Everglades is the gateway to the Caribbean.

Long Beach Area Convention and Visitors Bureau
www.golongbeach.com
One World Trade Ctr., Ste. 300
Long Beach, CA 90831
562/436-3645, ext. 100
Prime port from southern California to Mexico.

Vancouver Reservations
www.vancouver.com
100788 Harbourside Dr.

North Vancouver, BC
V7P 3R7 Canada
888/895-2870
The gateway to Alaska.

GOLF

Destinations

Kona-Kohala Coast
www.golf-kona.com
General information, schools and packages.

Kona-Kohala Chamber of Commerce
75-5737 Kuakini Hwy., Ste. 207
Kailua-Kona, HI 96740
808/329-1758

Maui
www.makena.com/golf.htm
maui-golf.com/
Two Web sites with course descriptions and booking.

Monterey Peninsula
Access Monterey Peninsula
www.mty.com/golf.html
General site with course information and links.

www.pebblebeach.com
Site for Pebble Beach resorts, with links for reservations.

www.travelguides.com/tours/monterey
General online travel guide with links.

Myrtle Beach
www.golfholiday.com
The main site for Myrtle Beach golf.

Orlando
www.orlando-golf.com
Course descriptions, on-line tee time reservations, photos and scorecards.

www.touristflorida.com/golf.html
Links to central Florida golf courses.

Palm Springs
Desert Golf Guide
www.desertgolfguide.com
Comprehensive listings.

Palm Springs Desert Resorts Convention and Visitors Bureau
www.palmspringsusa.com
www.palmspringsteetimes.com
69-930 Hwy. 111, Ste. 201
Rancho Mirage, CA 92270
760/770-1992, 760/770-9000, 800/967-3767, tee times 760/324-5012.

www.desertconnection.com
Information and links.

Pinehurst
Pinehurst Area Convention and Visitors Bureau
www.homeofgolf.com
Box 2270
Southern Pines, NC 28388
800/346-5362

San Diego

Golf San Diego
www.golfsandiego.com
Box 6215
San Diego, CA 92166
619/226-1749

San Diego Golf Pages
www.golfsd.com

Scottsdale

Scottsdale Golf and Lodging
www.scottsdalegolf.com
888/368-9171
Local golf packages and information.

www.scottsdale-golf.com
Course descriptions and tee times.

Schools

Golf Digest Schools
www.golfdigest.com/instruction/golfschools
5520 Park Ave.
Trumbull, CT 06611
800/243-6121

John Jacobs' Practical Golf Schools
www.jacobsgolf.com
7825 E. Redfield Rd.
Scottsdale, AZ 85260
480/991-8587, 800/472-5007

Nicklaus/Flick Golf Schools
www.nicklaus.com/instruction
11780 U.S. Hwy. 1
North Palm Beach, FL
3408-9809
800/642-5528

Pinehurst Golf Advantage School
www.pinehurst.com/golf/advantage.html
Box 4000, Carolina Vista
Pinehurst, NC 28374
800/795-4653

United States Schools of Golf
www.ussog.com
800/354-7515
Golf schools in 18 states.

GRANDPARENT TRAVEL

Foundation for Grandparenting
www.grandparenting.org
108 Farnham Rd.
Ojai, CA 93023

Specialty Travel Agencies

Grandtravel
www.grandtrvl.com
6900 Wisconsin Ave., Ste. 706
Chevy Chase, MD 20815
800/247-765, 301/986-0790

Rascals In Paradise
www.rascalsinparadise.com
One Daniel Burnham Ct., Ste. 105-C
San Francisco, CA 94109
415/921-7000

HOTELS, RESORTS, B&Bs

B&Bs

Bedandbreakfast.com
www.bedandbreakfast.com
Search more than 24,000 B&Bs and inns in the United States, Europe, and elsewhere by location, amenities, and other criteria.

Innplace.com
www.innplace.com
A directory of directories maintained by the Professional Association of Innkeepers International, a trade organization.

Karen Brown's Guides
www.karenbrown.com
The online presence of longtime inns expert Karen Brown showcases the hand-selected inns in her books, which Fodor's publishes.

Discounts

Roomsaver
www.roomsaver.com
4205 NW 6th St.
Gainesville, FL 32609
800/332-3948

Hotel Networks and Chains

American Hotel & Lodging Association
www.ahla.com
202/289-3100

Historic Hotels of America
www.nationaltrust.org/historic_hotels/
National Trust for Historic Preservation
1785 Massachusetts Ave., NW
Washington, DC 20036
800/678-8946, 202/588-6295

Leading Hotels of the World
www.lhw.com
99 Park Ave.
New York, NY 10016
800/223-6800

Small Luxury Hotels of the World
www.slh.com
14673 Midway Rd., Ste. 201
Addison, TX 75001
800/525-4800

PASSPORTS

Department of State
Office of Passport Services
Bureau of Consular Affairs
http://www.travel.state.gov/passport_services.html
The Web site has complete information and links to regional offices.

National Passport
Information Center
900/225-5674, 888/362-8668
Automated information for a fee. The 900 number costs 35 cents per minute for automated information, $1.05 per minute for operator-assisted calls (available 8:30–5:30 weekdays). The 888 number is a flat rate of $4.95/per call. You must pay by Visa, MasterCard, or American Express.

RAIL TRAVEL

American Association of Passenger Railway Car Owners
www.aaprco.com
630B Constitution Ave., NE
Washington, DC 20002
202/547-5696, 800/856-6876

Amtrak
www.amtrak.com
800/USA-RAIL

Durango-Silverton Narrow Gauge Railroad
www.durangorailway.com
479 Main Ave.
Durango, CO 81301
888/442-4222

Montana Rockies Rail Tours
www.montanarailtours.com
800/519-7245

Orient Express
www.orientexpresstrains.com
One Financial Centre Plaza, Ste. 500
10 Weybosset St.
Providence, RI 02903
800/524-2420
Luxury rail trips in Europe and beyond.

Rail Europe
www.raileurope.com
914/682-7456, 800/462-2577
European rail passes and Eurostar Channel Tunnel tickets.

Rail Travel Center
www.railtravelcenter.com
802/387-5812, 800/458-5394

RailsNW
www.railsnw.com
13215 SE Mill Pl. Blvd., #140
Vancouver, WA 98684
503/793-0523
Volunteer organization with database of bookable train trips nationwide.

Rocky Mountaineer Railtours
www.rockymountaineer.com
1150 Station St.
Vancouver, BC V6A 2X7
Canada
800/665-7245
Through Canada's Rockies.

VIA RailCanada
www.viarail.ca
416/366-8411, 888/842-7245 from Canada

www.cwrr.com/canpass /canpass.html
Independent site with links to many Canadian short- and long-haul passenger rail services, including the Algoma Central and others.

RENTAL HOMES

Vacation Rental Managers Association
www.vrma.com
Box 1202
Santa Cruz, CA 95061-1202
831/426-8762

REUNION PLANNING

On the Web

www.FamilyReunion .com

www.family-reunion .com

Planners

Reunion Network
www.reunionfriendly.com
2450 Hollywood Blvd.,
Ste. 504
Hollywood, FL 33020
800/225-5044

Family reunion planners across the U.S.

SHOPPING

Outlet Bound
www.outletbound.com
800/OUTLET-2
Guide to the largest U.S. outlet shopping malls.

SKIING

Colorado Ski Country USA
www.coloradoski.com
1507 Blake St.
Denver, CO 80202
303/837-0793
Association of 23 ski resorts in the state.

Cross-Country Ski Areas Association
259 Bolton Rd.
Winchester, NH 03470
603/239-4341

Ski Area Management
www.saminfo.com/assoc .htm
Beardsley Publishing
45 Main St. N.
Box 644
Woodbury, CT 06798
203/263-0888
Ski area management publication Web site, with links to many regional ski organizations.

Ski Europe
www.ski-europe.com
1535 West Loop S., Ste. 319
Houston, TX 77027
800/333-5533
Ski packages in Europe.

Ski the Rockies
www.skitherockies.com
800/291-2588
Ski packages to assorted
U.S. western resorts.

SPAS

Spa-Finders
www.spafinders.com
New York, NY
800/255-7727
The industry expert on spa
vacations, with a spa
specialty travel agency.

SPORTS AND OUTDOORS

Outward Bound
www.outwardbound.org
888/882-6863
Five wilderness outdoor-
skills schools and two
urban centers; team
building and personal
growth are focal points.

US Sports Camps
www.USSportsCamps.com
4470 Redwood Hwy.
San Rafael, CA 94903
800/645-3226, 415/459-0459
Nike-sponsored sports
camps in the United States
and Canada, some for
adults as well as juniors.

Worldwide Fishing Guide
www.worldwidefishing.com
2445 Morena Blvd., Ste. 204
San Diego CA 92110
619/275-7884, 800/545-5917
Information and links to
fishing lodges, guides, and
charter operators
worldwide.

THEME PARKS

Theme Park Insider
www.themeparkinsider.com
315 S. Sierra Madre Blvd.,
Ste. C
Pasadena, CA 91607
Details on, and links to,
theme parks across the
country.

Cedar Point
www.cedarpoint.com
419/627-2350

Dorney Park
www.dorneypark.com
610/395-3724

Hershey Park
www.hersheypark.com
800/437-7439

Paramount King's Dominion
www.kingsdominion.com
804/876-5561

Paramount King's Island
www.pki.com
800/288-0808

SeaWorld
www.seaworld.com
In Florida
800/327-2424
In California
619/226-3901

Six Flags
www.sixflags.com
Links to the Six Flags parks worldwide.

Universal Orlando
www.universalorlando.com
407/363-8000

Walt Disney World
www.disneyworld.com
407/824-4321

TOUR OPERATORS

Here are a few good ones to get you started.

Abercrombie and Kent
www.abercrombiekent.com
800/323-7308
Very upscale tours worldwide.

African Travel
www.africantravelinc.com
1100 E. Broadway
Glendale, CA 91205
818/507-7893 ext. 117,
800/421-8907

Backroads
www.backroads.com
801 Cedar St.
Berkeley, CA 94710-1800
510/527-1555, 800/462-2848
Upscale active trips; famed for bike tours.

Brendan Worldwide Vacations
www.brendantours.com
21625 Prairie St.
Chatsworth, CA 91311-5833
800/421-8446

Collette Vacations
www.collettevacations.com
162 Middle St.
Pawtucket, RI 2860
800/832-4656

Disney Travel
www.disney.go.com
800/327-2989
Disney park tickets and packages, Disney cruise vacations.

Eurovacations
www.eurovacations.com
877/471-3876
Packages in Europe.

Globus
www.globusandcosmos.com
5301 S Federal Circle
Littleton, CO 80123-8934
800/221-0090

Lindblad Expeditions
www.lindblad.com
720 Fifth Ave.
New York, NY 10019
800/397-3348
Upscale expeditions to remote spots.

Maupintour
www.maupintour.com
10650 W. Charleston Blvd.
Summerlin, NV 89135-1014
800/255-4266

Premier Tours
www.premiertours.com
217 S. 20th St.
Philadelphia, PA 19103
800/545-1910
A safari specialist headed by a former South African tourism official.

Tauck World Discovery
www.tauck.com
Box 5027
276 Post Rd. W
Westport, CT 06880
800/468-2825

Thomson Adventures
www.familyadventures.com
14 Mount Auburn St.
Watertown, MA 02472
800/262-6255
Adventures around the world for families.

Trafalgar Tours
www.TrafalgarTours.com
29-76 Northern Boulevard
Long Island City, NY 11101
800/854-0103

Travcoa
www.travcoa.com
2350 SE Bristol St.
Newport Beach, CA 92660
800/992-2003

Organizations

National Tour Association
www.nta.org
546 E. Main St.
Lexington, KY 40508
859/226-4444

US Tour Operators Association
www.ustoa.com
275 Madison Ave., Ste. 2014
New York, NY 10016
212/599-6599

TRAVEL AGENCIES

ASTA
The American Society of Travel Agents
www.astanet.com
1101 King St.
Alexandria, VA 22314
800/ASK-ASTA
Can refer you to specialty operators and member agencies in your area.

On the Web

Expedia
www.expedia.com

Orbitz
www.orbitz.com

Travelocity
www.travelocity.com

More Booking Online

Bestfares.com
Collects little-known offers; members have access to the best.

Cheaptickets.com
888/922-8849.
Research fares and availability, but call to confirm your fare is the lowest available.

Hotwire.com
You're offered a low fare; if you accept it, you're told the carrier and flight information.

Lowestfare.com
Uses American Airlines' Sabre system.

OneTravel.com

Qixo.com
Searches 20 top travel Web sites.

TRAVEL INSURANCE

Access America
www.accessamerica.com
800/284-8300

The Berkely Group
www.berkely.com
100 Garden City Plaza
Box 9366
Garden City, NY 11530
800/645-2424

Travel Guard International
www.travel-guard.com
800/826-4919

Travel Insured
www.travelinsured.com
800/243-3174
Travelers Insurance is the underwriter.

Travelex
www.travelex-insurance.com
800/797-4515
The former Mutual of Omaha, now part of Thomas Cook.

VISITOR INFORMATION

Resorts OnLine
www.resortsonline.com
30 E. 68 St.
New York, NY 10021
212/744-6586
Collection of resort hotels and resort destinations as well as topical links for vacations that involve golf, skiing, scuba diving, horseback riding, fishing, spa, casinos, safaris, lakes, castles and chateaux, and the beach.

www.towd.com
Links to official tourist offices in the United States and around the world.

Destinations Abroad

Argentina
Secretary of Tourism (Sectur)
www.sectur.com

Aruba
Aruba Tourism Authority
www.aruba.com
1000 Harbor Blvd.
Weehawken, NJ 07087
201/330-0800,
800/TO-ARUBA

Australia
Australian Tourist Commission
www.australia.com
2049 Century Park E,
Ste. 1920
Los Angeles, CA 90067
800/369-6863

Austria
Austrian National Tourist Office
www.austria-tourism.at/us
500 Fifth Ave., Ste. 800
New York, NY 10110
212/575-7723

Barbados
Barbados Tourism Authority
www.barbados.org
800 Second Ave.
New York, NY 10017
212/986-6516, 800/221-9831

Brazil
Minister of Sport and Tourism
www.embratur.com

Canada
Canada Tourism Commission
www.travelcanada.ca
877/822-6232

Caribbean
Caribbean Hotel Association
www.caribbeanhotels.org
1000 Ponce De Leon Blvd.
San Juan, Puerto Rico 00907
787/725-9139
Links to hotel groups on individual islands.

Caribbean Tourism
Organization
www.doitcaribbean.com
80 Broad St.
New York, NY 10004
212/635-9530

Costa Rica
Costa Rica Tourism and
Travel Bureau
www.costaricabureau.com
SJO 667
Box 025240
Miami, FL 33102
506/296-7074 in Costa Rica

Ecuador
Ministry of Tourism
www.ecuaventura.com

Embassy of Ecuador
2535 15th St. NW
Washington, DC 20009
202/234-7200

Europe
European Travel
Commission
www.visiteurope.com
One Rockefeller Plaza,
Ste. 214
New York, NY 10020
212/218-1200
Information regarding 30
European member countries
and links to their sites.

France
French Government
Tourist Office
www.francetourism.com
www.franceguide.com
444 Madison Ave., 16th floor
New York, NY 10022
212/838-7800

Galapagos
Galapagos Chamber of
Tourism
www.galapagoschamberof
tourism.org

Great Britain
British Tourist Authority
www.travelbritain.org
551 Fifth Ave., Ste. 701
New York, NY 10176
212/986-2266

Greece
Greek National Tourist
Organization
www.gnto.gr
645 Fifth Ave.
New York, NY 10022
212/421-5777

Ireland
Irish Tourist Board
www.irelandvacations.com
345 Park Ave.
New York, NY 10154
212/418-0800

Italy
Italian Government Tourist
Office
www.italiantourism.com
630 Fifth Ave.
New York, NY 10111
212/245-5618

Jamaica
Jamaica Tourist Board
www.jamaicatravel.com
801 Second Ave.
New York, NY 10017
212 856-9727, 800/526-2522

Mexico
Mexican Government
Tourist Office
www.visitmexico.com
405 Park Ave.
New York, NY 10022
212/755-7261

Pacific
Pacific Asia Travel
Association
www.pata.org
Latham Square Building
1611 Telegraph Ave.,
Ste. 1515
Oakland, CA 94612
510/625-2055
Links to information on
Asian member tourist
countries.

Scandinavia
Scandinavian Tourist Offices
www.goscandinavia.com
655 Third Ave.
New York, NY 10017
212/949-2333
Information on, and links to,
Denmark, Sweden, Finland,
Norway, and Iceland.

South Africa
South African Tourism
www.southafricantourism.com
500 Fifth Ave., Ste. 2040
New York, NY 10110
212/730-2929

St. Barthelemy
Office du Tourisme
www.st-barths.com
Quai General de Gaulle
Gustavia, 97133
St. Barthelemy, French
West Indies
590/0 5 90 27 87 27

Switzerland
Switzerland Tourism
www.myswitzerland.com
608 Fifth Ave.
New York, NY 10020
877/794-8037

Tahiti
Tahiti Travel Planners
www.gotahiti.com
New Millennium Travel
461 Durand NE Ste. 100
Atlanta, GA 30307
800/772-9231
A specialty travel agency.

Spain
Tourist Office of Spain
www.okspain.org
666 Fifth Ave. 35th Floor
New York, NY 10103
212/265-8822

USA Favorites

General
City Spin
www.cityspin.com
800/275-5895

Information on, and links to, 35 major U.S. cities.
www.normanpickell.com/links_travelusa.htm
Links to many state tourism sites.

Alaska

Alaska Travel Industry Association
www.travelalaska.com
2600 Cordova St., Ste. 201
Anchorage, AK 99503

Arizona

Arizona Office of Tourism
www.arizonaguide.com
2702 N. 3rd St., Ste. 4015
Phoenix, AZ 85007
602/230-7733, 888/520-3434

Greater Phoenix Convention and Visitors Bureau
www.phoenixcvb.com
One Arizona Center
400 E. Van Buren St, Ste. 600
Phoenix, AZ 85004
602/254-6500

Arkansas

Arkansas Department of Parks and Tourism
www.arkansas.com
One Capitol Mall
Little Rock, AR 72201
800/628-8725

California

California Travel and Tourism Commission
www.gocalif.ca.gov
801 K St. Ste. 1600
Sacramento, CA 95814
916/322-3424

Huntington Beach Conference and Visitors Bureau
www.hbvisit.com
417 Main St.
Huntington Beach, CA 92648-5131
714/969-3492, 800/729-6232

Los Angeles Convention and Visitors Bureau
www.lacvb.com
633 W. Fifth St., Ste. 6000
Los Angeles, CA 90071
213/624-7300

Monterey Peninsula Visitors and Convention Bureau
www.monterey.com
One Portola Plaza
Monterey, CA 93940
831/649-1770

Newport Beach Conference and Visitors Bureau
www.newportbeach-cvb.com
3300 W. Coast Highway
Newport Beach, CA 92663
800/942-6278

San Diego Convention and Visitors Bureau
www.sdcvb.org
401 B St., Ste. 1400
San Diego, CA 92101-4237
619/236-1212

San Francisco Convention
and Visitors Bureau
www.sfvisitor.org
201 Third St., Ste. 900
San Francisco, CA 94103
415/283-0177, 888/782-9673
for hotel reservations

Santa Barbara Convention
and Visitors Bureau
www.santabarbaraca.com
1601 Anacapa St.
Santa Barbara, CA
93101-1909
805/966-9222, 800/549-5133

Colorado
Colorado Tourism Office
www.colorado.com
1625 Broadway, Ste. 1700
Denver, CO 80202
800/265-6723

Denver Metro Convention
and Visitors Bureau
www.denver.org
1555 California St., Ste. 300
Denver, CO 80210
303/892-1112, 800/462-5280

District of Columbia
DC Committee to Promote
Washington
www.washington.org
1212 New York Ave., NW,
Ste. 200
Washington, DC 20005
202/789-7000, 800/422-8644

Florida
Visit Florida
www.flausa.com
888/735-2872

Information from the state
hotel and motel association
and the Florida Association
of RV Parks and
Campgrounds.

Greater Miami Convention
and Visitors Bureau
www.miamiandbeaches
.com
701 Brickell Ave., Ste. 2700
Miami, FL 33131
305/539-3100, 800/933-8448

Orlando/Orange County
Convention and Visitors
Bureau
www.orlandoinfo.com
6700 Forum Dr.
Orlando, FL 32821
407/363-5872
www.go2orlando.com

Georgia
Georgia Tourism
www.georgia.org/
285 Peachtree Center Ave.,
Ste. 1000
Atlanta, GA 30303
800/847-4842

Hawaii
Hawaii Visitors and
Convention Bureau
www.gohawaii.com
2270 Kalakaua Ave.,
Ste. 801
Honolulu, HI 96815
808/923-1811, 800/464-2924

Idaho
Idaho Recreation and
Tourism
www.visitid.org

700 West State St.,
Box 83720
Boise, ID 83720-0093
208/334-2470, 800/842-5858

Illinois
Illinois Bureau of Tourism
www.enjoyillinois.com
100 W. Randolph St.,
Ste. 3-400
Chicago IL 60601
312/814-4733, 800/226-6632

Chicago Convention and
Visitors Bureau
www.chicago.il.org
2301 S. Lake Shore Dr.
Chicago, IL 60616
312/567-8500

Indiana
Department of Commerce,
Tourism Development
Division
www.enjoyindiana.com
1 N. Capitol, Ste. 700
Indianapolis, IN
46204-2288
317/232-8860, 888/365-6946

Kentucky
Kentucky Department of
Travel Development
www.kytourism.com
Box 2011
Frankfort, KY 40602
800/225-8747

Louisiana
Louisiana Office of Tourism
www.louisianatravel.com
Box 94291
Baton Rouge LA 70804-9291
225/342-8100, 225/342-8119,
800/334-8626

Lafayette Convention and
Visitors Bureau
www.lafayettetravel.com
Box 52066
Lafayette, LA 70505
800/346-1958
Information on Cajun
country.

New Orleans Metropolitan
Convention and Visitors
Bureau
www.neworleanscvb.com
1520 Sugar Bowl Dr.
New Orleans, LA 70112
504/566-5011, 800/672-6124

Maine
Maine Tourism Association
www.mainetourism.com
325B Water St.
Hallowell, ME 04347-2300
207/623-0363, 800/533-9595

Maryland
Maryland Office of
Tourism Development
www.mdisfun.org
217 E. Redwood St.
Baltimore, MD 21202
410/767-3400, 800/634-7386

Massachusetts
Massachusetts Office of
Travel and Tourism
www.massvacation.com
10 Park Plaza, Ste. 4510
Boston, MA 02116
617/973-8500, 800/227-6277

Greater Boston Convention
and Visitors Bureau
www.bostonusa.com
Two Copley Pl. Ste. 105
Boston, MA 02116
617/536-4100, 888/733-2678

Cape Cod Chamber of
Commerce
www.capecodchamber.org
307 Main St., Ste. 2
Hyannis, MA 02601
508/862-0700

Martha's Vineyard
Chamber of Commerce
www.mvy.com
Box 1698
Vineyard Haven, MA 02568
508/693-0085

Nantucket Island Chamber
of Commerce
www.nantucketchamber.org
48 Main St.
Nantucket, MA 02554
508/228-1700

Michigan
Travel Michigan
www.michigan.org
Box 30226
Lansing MI 48909-7726
888/784-7328

Minnesota
Minnesota Office of
Tourism
www.exploreminnesota.com
100 Metro Square, 121 7th
Pl. E.
St. Paul, MN 55101
651/296-5029, 800/657-3700

Mississippi
Mississippi Division of
Tourism
www.visitmississippi.org
Box 849
Jackson, MS 39205
800/927-6378, 601/359-3297

Mississippi Gulf Coast
Convention and Visitors
Bureau
www.gulfcoast.org/mgccvb
Box 6128
Gulfport, MS 39506-6128
888/467-4853

Missouri
Missouri Division of
Tourism
www.missouritourism.org
Box 1055
Jefferson City, MO 65102
573/751-4133, 800/877-1234

Branson Convention and
Visitors Bureau
www.bransonchamber.com
Box 1897
Branson, MO 65615
800/214-3661

Convention and Visitors
Bureau of Greater Kansas
City
http://www.visitkc.com
1100 Main, Ste. 2550
Kansas City, MO 64105
816/691-3800, 800/767-7700

St. Louis Convention and
Visitors Commission
www.st-louis-cvc.com

One Metropolitan Square,
Ste. 1100
St. Louis, MO 63102
800/325-7962

Montana
Travel Montana
www.travel.state.mt.us
Box 200533
1424 9th Ave.
Helena, MT 59620
406/444-2654, 800/847-4868

Nevada
Las Vegas Convention and
Visitors Authority
www.lasvegas24hours.com
3150 Paradise Rd.
Las Vegas, NV 89109
702/892-0711

New Hamsphire
New Hampshire Division
of Travel and Tourism
Development
www.visitnh.gov
172 Pembroke Rd.
Box 1856
Concord, NH 03302-1856
800/386-4664

New Jersey
New Jersey Commerce and
Economic Growth
Commission
www.state.nj.us/travel
Box 820
Trenton, NJ 08625-0820
609/777-0885, 800/847-4865

Atlantic City Convention
and Visitors Authority
www.atlanticcitynj.com
2314 Pacific Ave.
Atlantic City, NJ 08401
609/348-7100, 888/228-4748

New Mexico
New Mexico Department
of Tourism
www.newmexico.org
800/733-6396 ext. 0643

Santa Fe Convention and
Visitors Bureau
www.santafe.org
Box 909
Santa Fe, 87504-0909
505/955-6200, 800/777-CITY

Santa Fe County Chamber
of Commerce
www.santafechamber.com
510 North Guadalupe,
Ste. N
Santa Fe, NM 87501
(Also Box 1928, Santa Fe,
NM 87504)
505/983-7317, 505-/988-3279

New York
New York State Division of
Tourism
www.iloveny.com
Box 2603
Albany, NY 12220-0603
518/474-4116, 800/225-5697

NYC & Co.
www.nycvisit.com
810 7th Ave. 3rd Floor
New York, NY 10019
212/484-1200
The New York City
convention and visitors
bureau.

North Carolina
North Carolina Division
of Tourism
www.visitnc.com
301 N. Wilmington St.
Raleigh, NC 27601
919/733-4171, 800/847-4862

Outer Banks Chamber of
Commerce Office
www.outerbankschamber
.com
Box 1757
101 Town Hall Dr.
Kill Devil Hills, NC 27948
252/441-8144

Ohio
Ohio Division of Travel
and Tourism
www.ohiotourism.com
Box 1001
Columbus, OH 43216-1001
614/466-8844, 614/466-6744,
800/282-5393

Oregon
Oregon Tourism
Commission
Oregon Economic and
Community Development
Department
www.traveloregon.com
775 Summer St. NE
Salem, OR 97301-1280
800/547-7842

Pennsylvania
Pennsylvania Office of
Travel, Tourism, and Film
www.state.pa.us/visit
800/847-4872

Philadelphia Convention
and Visitors Bureau
www.pcvb.org
1515 Market St. #2020
Philadelphia, PA 19102
215/636-3300, 800/225-5745

Greater Pittsburgh
Convention and Visitors
Bureau
www.visitpittsburgh.com
425 Sixth Ave., 30th floor
Pittsburgh, PA 15219-1834
412/281-7711, 800/359-0758

South Carolina
South Carolina
Department of Parks,
Recreation and Tourism
www.discoversouthcarolina
.com
888/727-6453

Hilton Head Island Visitor
and Convention Bureau
www.hiltonheadisland.org
Box 5647
Hilton Head Island, SC
29938
843/785-3673, 800/523-3373

Myrtle Beach
www.myrtlebeachlive.com
Myrtle Beach Area
Hospitality Association
www.mbhospitality.org
Box 1303
Myrtle Beach, SC 29578
843/626-9668

Myrtle Beach Area
Chamber of Commerce
Convention and Visitors
Bureau
www.mbchamber.com/cvb
1200 N. Oak St.
800/356-3016, ext. 199

South Dakota
South Dakota Department
of Tourism
Capitol Lake Plaza
711 E. Wells Ave.
c/o 500 E. Capitol Ave.
Pierre, SD 57501-5070
605/773-3301, 800/732-5682

Tennessee
Tennessee Department of
Tourist Development
www.tourism.state.tn.us
Rachael Jackson Bldg.,
5th floor
320 Sixth Ave. N.
Nashville, TN 37243
615/741-2159, 800/462-8366

Nashville Area Convention
and Visitors Bureau
211 Commerce St., Ste. 100
Nashville, TN 37201
800/657-6910, 615/743-3000

Texas
Department of Commerce,
Tourism Division
www.traveltex.com
Box 141009
Austin, TX 78714
512/486-5900, 800/888-8839

Austin Convention and
Visitors Bureau
www.austintexas.org
201 E. 2nd St.
Austin, TX 78701
512/474-5171, 800/926-2282

Corpus Christi Convention
and Visitors Bureau
www.corpuschristi-tx-cvb
.org
1201 N. Shoreline
Corpus Christi, TX 78401
361/881-1888, 800/678-6232,
800/766-2322

Dallas Convention and
Visitors Bureau
www.dallascvb.com
325 N. St. Paul St.
Dallas, TX 75201
214/571-1000, 214/571-1300,
800/232-5527

Fort Worth Convention
and Visitors Bureau
www.fortworth.com
415 Throckmorton
Fort Worth, TX 76102
800/433-5747, 817/336-8791

San Antonio Convention
and Visitors Bureau
www.sanantoniocvb.com

Mailing Address
Box 2277
San Antonio, TX 78298

Street Address
203 S. St. Mary's St.
San Antonio, Texas 78205
210/207-6700, 800/447-3372

Utah

Utah Travel Council
www.utah.com
Council Hall/Capitol Hill
Salt Lake City, UT
84114-1396
801/538-1030, 800/883-4386

Ski Utah
www.skiutah.com
150 W. 500 S.
Salt Lake City, UT 84101
(801) 534-1779

Vermont

Vermont Chamber of
Commerce
www.vtchamber.com
Box 37
Montpelier, VT 05601
802/223-3443

Vermont Department of
Tourism and Marketing
www.1-800-vermont.com
6 Baldwin St., Drawer 33
Montpelier, VT 05633-1301
800/837-6668

Virginia

Virginia Tourism
Corporation
www.virginia.org
901 East Byrd St.
Richmond, VA 23219
800/248-4833, 800/321-3244

Washington State

Washington State Tourism
Division
www.experiencewashington.com
Box 42500
Olympia, WA 98504-2500
360/725-5052

Seattle–King County
Convention and Visitors
Bureau
www.seeseattle.org
520 Pike St., Ste. 1300
Seattle, WA 98101
206/461-5800

West Virginia

West Virginia Division of
Tourism
www.callwva.com
90 MacCorkle Ave., SW
S. Charleston, WV 25303
304/558-2200, 800/225-5982

VOLUNTEER PROGRAMS

Global Volunteers

www.globalvolunteers.org
375 East Little Canada Rd.
St. Paul, MN 55117
651/407-6100, 800/487-1074

Habitat for Humanity

www.habitat.org
121 Habitat St.
Americus, GA 31709
229/924-6935, ext. 2551 or 2552

Volunteers For Peace

www.vfp.org
1034 Tiffany Rd.
Belmont, VT 05730
802/259-2759